THE ENGLISH
POETIC MIND

THE ENGLISH POETIC MIND

BY

CHARLES WILLIAMS

New York

RUSSELL & RUSSELL

1963

FIRST PUBLISHED IN 1932

REISSUED, 1963, BY RUSSELL & RUSSELL, INC.

L. C. CATALOG CARD NO: 63—15188

PRINTED IN THE UNITED STATES OF AMERICA

PREFACE

THE following essays are based on two convictions: (1) that *Troilus and Cressida* is of a great deal more importance in a study of Shakespeare than has generally been allowed, (2) that the central crisis of *Troilus* is in direct poetic relation to the culminating crisis in Wordsworth's account of his own history in the *Prelude*. From these convictions I went on to consider whether that crisis had any parallels in the work of the other English poets, and whether it might, not unreasonably, be related to the Satan of Milton, compared with the Nightingale of Keats, and contrasted with the Lancelot of Tennyson. Upon this subject it would have been possible to write a book either of five hundred or of two hundred pages; I chose two hundred with equal reluctance and decision.

I have called it the *English Poetic Mind* rather than the *English Poetic Genius*, because the word genius, in that context, might be supposed to have reference rather to 'English' than to 'Poetic'; to allude to the feelings which (as Sir Arthur Quiller Couch has suggested) should be aroused in us when we stand by the tomb of the Black Prince in Canterbury Cathedral rather than to those which are aroused by the reading of *Henry V*. With the patriotism of Shakespeare and Milton and the rest I have nothing to do; only with their poetry. But to omit the geographical limitation altogether would have been too bold; the present title sounds more like the tentative suggestion which the book is meant to offer.

Even so, all the English poets are not here: Chaucer, Spenser, Dryden, for example. I can only plead that two hundred pages are better than five hundred, and that to do more than is here done would have meant the five hundred: it would have had to be a full volume with notes and appendices and longer quotations and digressions and defences and explanations all complete. Aristotle on tragedy and De Quincey on power and Coleridge on poetry and everybody on Shakespeare and almost everybody on Keats would have had to come in. To the general critical intelligence of our own times I owe of course a profound debt, poorly as this study may seem to pay any of it; to the critical authority of the past a proper obedience. But on the central question of *Troilus* I am not conscious of owing any particular debt at all. Something of the possibility I tried to put into verse in my *Myth of Shakespeare*; it is here defined in prose.

Of one fact I am a little proud. The suggestions made here are quite unexclusive. Shakespeare, Milton, and Wordsworth may have been moved by any personal cause or aiming at any moral or metaphysical purpose conceivable—it does not matter, I have been concerned with the poetry only as it exists, and with its interrelation. Even the prose statements which the poets themselves made about their poetry are omitted. Criticism has done so much to illuminate the poets, and yet it seems, with a few exceptions, both of the past and the present, still not sufficiently to relate the poets to the poets, to explain poetry by poetry. Yet in the end what other criterion have we? Wordsworth's poetry is

likely to explain Shakespeare's poetry much better
than we can, because poetry is a thing *sui generis*.
It explains itself by existing. There has been a great
deal too much talking of what the poets *mean*. They
also are mortal; they also express themselves badly
sometimes; they also sometimes fail to discover quite
finally the exact scope of their desire. We can enjoy
ourselves talking about them, of course; the multitudinous printed chat of generations lies behind and
around us. But *criticism*—is it being stupid to say
that in the end the poets themselves must do that
also for us? We know so little unless they tell us;
we feel as they direct us; we are disordered and astray
unless they govern us. Poetry is a good game—let
us take it lightly. But it is also 'liberty and power'—
let us take it seriously. *Ad maiorem poetarum gloriam*
—there is but one ascription more worthy than that,
and in the tradition of Christendom it was amid a
cloud of songs as well as of seraphs that the Divine
Word accepted incarnation.

C. W.

CONTENTS

I

A NOTE ON GREAT POETRY

THE word 'poetry' is generally used in one of two senses. It either means the whole mass of amusing and delightful stuff written in verse, or it is restricted to those greater lines, stanzas, or poems which are comparatively rare even in the work of the great poets. There is no certain method of deciding on these last, except by personal experience (which is not quite reliable) or by authority—the judgement of sensitive readers over many years. There is no way of discovering how the thing is done, nor exactly how a great line produces its effect. But it is to some extent possible to see what the difference is between the lesser kind of verse and the greater.

Wordsworth in the *Prelude* (1, 149–57), defines three things as necessary for the writing of poetry. They are (i) 'the vital soul', (ii) 'general truths', (iii) 'external things—Forms, images'. With these possessions in himself he feels prepared for his own 'arduous work'. The distinction exists for the reader as well. The third necessity ('aids Of less regard') is an obvious part of most poetry: it includes metaphors, similes, comparisons; even the story, and the persons in narrative or dramatic verse or the hypothetical speaker, the individual poet, in lyric. These things are 'needful to build up a poet's praise', and at their most exquisite they play an important part in the whole. But the greatest poetry can exist without them. 'A rose-red city, half as old as Time' is a lovely line. It stops at being that.

'General truths'—'subordinate helpers of the living mind'—on the other hand, though more important, are less reliable aids: for they have a way of pretending to be the living mind, the 'vital soul' itself. Some of the poets—Longfellow, Tennyson, Wordsworth himself—appear occasionally to have thought they were writing poetry when they were merely communicating general truths, or what appeared to them to be so. *The Excursion*, as opposed to the *Prelude*, gives examples of this; although even the *Excursion*, if a reader will only accept the conditions it postulates, as he is ready to accept the plot of *King Lear*, may turn out to be a better poem than is often supposed. Perhaps, however, such a couplet as Hamlet's yields the best example of general truths, which, adequately expressed, delight us almost as much by rational as by poetic strength—

> Imperious Caesar, dead and turned to clay,
> Might stop a hole to keep the wind away.

But what then is the 'vital soul', without which the forms and images and general truths lack something? It is 'genius'; it is 'poetry'. But that takes us no farther. It cannot be merely the relation of labials and gutturals, or the play of stresses and pauses. These are, in another shape, the 'forms and images'. It cannot be the diction—however exact or unexpected; that is but a general truth. All such things are 'subordinate helpers of the living mind', which must itself use them for its own purpose. What does that mind do in *Hyperion* which it does not do in *Horatius*? why is Pope a greater poet than Prior or Praed?

Poetry, one way or another, is 'about' human experience; there is nothing else that it can be about. But to whatever particular human experience it alludes, it is not that experience. Love poetry is poetry, not love; patriotic poetry is poetry, not patriotism; religious poetry is poetry, not religion. But good poetry does something more than allude to its subject; it is related to it, and it relates us to it.

> Through the sad heart of Ruth when, sick for home,
>   She stood in tears amid the alien corn:

those lines relate us to an experience of exile. They awake in us a sense of exile; more accurately, a realization of our own capacity for enduring exile.

> Let this immortal life, where'er it comes,
>   Walk in a cloud of loves and martyrdoms;

that awakes in us—not certainly love and sacrifice, or love and sacrifice would be easier things than they seem to be. But it does awake a sense that we are capable of love and sacrifice. It reminds us of a certain experience, and by its style it awakes a certain faculty for that experience. We are told of a thing; we are made to feel as if that thing were possible to us; and we are so made to feel it—whatever the thing may be, joy or despair or what not—that our knowledge is an intense satisfaction to us; and this knowledge and this satisfaction are for some period of time complete and final; and this knowledge, satisfaction, and finality are all conveyed through the medium of words, the concord of which is itself a delight to the senses. This sensuous apprehension of our satisfied capacities for some experience or other is poetry of the finest kind.

Lesser verse does not do so much. It may remind us that we have some capacity or other, but it does not communicate a delighted sense of it, nor therefore can it join that sense to the equally delighted sense of words. *The Armada* is, in its way, an exciting and pleasing piece of writing. But it does not arouse in us a sense of our capacity for staunch patriotism; it excites by reminding us that there is a capacity for staunch patriotism.

Bolingbroke in *Richard II* talks very beautifully about exile. But we are much more inclined to think as we read, 'That is how I should like to talk if I were ever exiled'; we are reminded of our capacity for beautifully expressing our grief at exile rather than of our capacity for suffering exile—that is with Ruth more than with Bolingbroke. Horatius confronting Lars Porsena, FitzJames confronting Roderick Dhu, do not convey a sense of man's capacity for heroism; they at most remind us that man has a capacity for heroism.

> Round turned he, as not deigning
>   Those heathen ranks to see;
> Naught spake he to Lars Porsena,
>   To Sextus naught spake he.

How jolly to behave like that! The pretence of such behaviour is agreeably invoked by those admirable lines. For they are, in their degree, admirable; it is another, and a moral, question how far we allow them to deceive us: they do not try to. They thrill us, and thrills are good, only one cannot live by thrills. But

> So spake the Seraph Abdiel, faithful found,
> Among the faithless faithful only he;

Among innumerable false unmoved,
Unshaken, unseduced, unterrified.

It would not be so easy to behave like *that*. Our capacity for heroism is stirred—or at least our desire for, our recognition of, that capacity. But can we desire or recognize something of which we are *entirely* incapable? 'Hadst thou not found me, thou couldst not be seeking me', said Christ to one of the mystics; and the same thing is true of the faculties awakened by poetry.

Certainly this awakening, this communication, is rather a result than a motive. Tolstoy declared that art existed wherever there was a conscious communication of emotion. Tolstoy was a great man and a great novelist; but we must not stress that admirable definition as if the poet primarily, in the very definition of his work, demanded an audience. If it is so, then our sensation that the great things of poetry exist purely and simply in their own right, and independently of man, is false. It may be; sensations are doubtful things and prove nothing unless we choose that they shall. But, putting that choice aside, it is surely true that the chief impulse of a poet is, not to communicate a thing to others, but to shape a thing, to make an immortality for its own sake. He often writes from other motives, no doubt; Pope probably wished to communicate his emotions about Addison, and Shelley his about the death of Keats. But did Keats really want first of all to communicate his emotions about a Nightingale? or Shakespeare his about Macbeth? Did Shakespeare primarily want to make *us* feel what a murderer's heart was like? It is inconceivable; he primarily wanted that heart to be.

Certainly if no one, no one *ever*, reads a poet, if no one cares for him, he may leave off writing. But that is the weakness of his nature, as Milton said. Fame is 'the last infirmity of noble mind'. Infirmity. But a poet might be content to communicate anonymously? Even so, he wants his work to produce a social effect. Does the poet, *qua* poet, care whether his work has a social effect? *Incredibile; nec crediderim nisi Tolstoy*—and not even then.

But, leaving this dispute and returning to the nature of poetry, we come to a further division. If it is true that the minor poets describe heroism or love or exile or what not, and the major poets arouse in us an actual sense of our own faculties for heroism and love and exile, what of the greatest? If the Marlowes are greater than the Macaulays, why are the Miltons greater still? What is it that makes us instinctively introduce the idea of relative values?

In so far as the poets can be hierarchized, it can only be done by two classifications (i) quantity, (ii) quality. The smallest poet who has written one good line—say, Dean Burgon, with his 'rose-red city'—is, so far, equal to any other poet who has written a good line—even Shakespeare. He arouses in us a capacity of enjoying a particular picture, by placing a picture before us which we do actually enjoy. It is delightful to have such a thing in our minds—and that is that. We are obliged—deeply obliged—by the Dean, but if he can only provide us with one picture whereas some other poet can provide us with twenty, we must regard the second poet as more important for us; unless we have a peculiar passion for rose-red cities.

But quality is more important, and the question of quality very soon becomes a question of complexity. Of the development of that poetic complexity this book is meant to be a small consideration, and there is /no need to forestall it here. The rose-red city becomes inhabited by human emotions, and its poetry disappears under the stress of theirs. In turn the single poignant utterances give place to lines which sum up states of involved experience. Such lines may in themselves appear to draw nearer to or to pass farther from the complexity which they describe. But either way they are aware of it, whether in increase or decrease. The decrease is a decrease from something that has been. Neither increase nor decrease is better than the other; they are merely two poetic methods of dealing with very profound and almost universal apprehensions of our faculties of experience. 'Absent thee from felicity awhile' is a very great and complex line; it has two worlds of experience in it; it calls up the whole idea of, the whole of our capacity for, felicity only to meet it with our capacity for rejection, and it unifies, it prolongs, both ideas in the 'awhile'. If Hamlet had been asking Horatio to reject felicity for ever, if he had wanted him to be quite final about it, we should have had a very different line, and one which implied a decrease of complexity. 'Life is a tale . . . signifying nothing' tends towards a decrease of complexity. But it must be allowed also that it implies the complexity it leaves behind; the word 'signifying' with its multitudinous associations does that. Compare the words 'awhile' and 'nothing' and you have the two different states towards which the greatest poetry tends. Satan in *Paradise Lost* remains a highly charged and complex figure. But Lear is becoming a transmuted and simple figure.

Our capacities then for some sort of general experience of the world are awakened by the greater masters. As far as poetry is concerned it does not matter what that capacity is: Macbeth is as poetically effective as Samson. Both express our sense of a faculty for taking in many experiences as a whole, for knowing and enjoying them, for knowing and enjoying them in the exquisite sensuous delight of words. Anybody who can cause us to do that is a great poet.

II

'THE GROWTH OF A POET'S MIND'

THERE is in English poetry only one long study of the poetic mind. That study is the *Prelude or the Growth of a Poet's Mind*. 'A Poet' to most readers means Wordsworth; to Wordsworth himself it would certainly have meant Wordsworth. But in the course of that account he describes at least one crisis which has been treated, in a very different way, both by Shakespeare and Milton, which has been approached by other poets and avoided by yet others. It seems worth while, therefore, to note once more, very briefly, the chief points in that growth and development, in order that its most important moment may be kept clearly in mind. Most of the books upon the *Prelude* consider it in relation to Wordsworth, and Wordsworth too often in relation to Nature, the sensationalist philosophy, Godwinism, and mysticism. He is comparatively rarely considered as a poet whose value lies in, and only in, the poems he writes—not in what he means by them. *The Prelude* has yet to be fully considered in relation to general poetry, and that would probably best be done by an edition of the poem annotated for that purpose with parallel passages from other poets. The present quotations are rather reminders of themselves than evidence of any theory. Wordsworth wrote the *Prelude* as a prelude, an account of his own preparation for what he was about to do; it was to invigorate him, to 'fix the wavering balance' of his mind, to 'spur' him on. It is therefore largely an account of his own experiences, and those experiences were for him 'Nature' and Man. He was inclined to stress the necessity of 'Nature' for poets; he sympathizes with Coleridge for not having had his own advantages, for being 'debarred from Nature's living images', and regrets that his influence had not soothed Coleridge's youthful unhappiness. But the times at which Wordsworth's own personal opinions enter into the *Prelude* are fairly clear, and we need not take those periods too seriously. The authority of poetry is only present when great poetry is present; poetry in the *Prelude* is never far away, but it is not always active.

It is Wordsworth's personal opinion—he offers it as his 'best conjecture'—that the poetic spirit is natural to every man. The passage in the 1805–6 version is more metaphysical than in the 1850. There it is explained that the Babe, gathering 'passion from his Mother's eye', is eager to combine 'in one appearance' all the apparently detached elements and parts of 'the same object'. The baby, one gathers, having vaguely realized that his mother is unity, is anxious to recognize unity in every object. This 'conjecture' Wordsworth afterwards removed, but it remains of interest for it suggests how the sensational apprehension of completeness in one being excites the poetic mind to see such a completeness in other separate objects. Each one is separate, yet each is complete, each is a whole. This is the first small result of that power which works afterwards to create in poetry 'Composure and ennobling Harmony'.

Secondly, from its sense of its mother, from its

'most apprehensive habitude', and from the 'sensations which have been derived' from its knowledge
of its mother—from all these the baby derives 'a
virtue which irradiates and exalts' all other objects.
Its mind already works 'in alliance' with the works
which it beholds; it is at once creator and receiver.
It is these two characteristics which mark the small
poet—(a) its passion for unifying (b) its powers and
quickness to co-operate with 'the active universe'.
But this 'first poetic spirit' is, in most, afterwards
'abated or suppressed'; in some it is 'pre-eminent
till death'. These last presumably are the poets—
the poets and the poetry to whom Wordsworth so
often applies the words 'Powers' and 'Power'. For
example: of books and their writers (v. 218)

> speak of them as Powers
> For ever to be hallowed;

Of words in tuneful order (v. 556),

> sweet
> For their own sake, a passion, and a power;

Of the shell that was poetry (v. 107),

> The other that was a god, yea, many gods,
> Had voices more than all the winds, with power;

and so also (v. 595):

> Visionary power
> Attends the motions of the viewless winds,
> Embodied in the mystery of words.

Of imagination (vi. 592)

> here the Power so called,
> Through sad incompetence of human speech,
> That awful Power, rose from the mind's abyss:

and there are other instances.

This Power, Wordsworth held, was of the first importance to man. He left the statement unaltered, or, if anything, slightly enforced, through all the modifications of the *Prelude*. Some things he unsaid, but *that* he never unsaid. In Book V is the vision of the Arab, carrying geometry and poetry, escaping on a camel from the deluge and the floods that are to destroy mankind; and to this vision Wordsworth says that he often deliberately returned, consciously changing the Arab to a 'gentle dweller in the desert', seized with a noble madness; consciously regarding him and his quest of salvation for poetry with reverence, and identifying himself with him. In such a madness, such a dream, is reason. There are enough people on earth to take in charge

> Their wives, their children, and their virgin loves,
> Or whatsoever else the heart holds dear.

Wordsworth himself, in such a catastrophe will, with his own dreamed fanatic, abandon everything else to save poetry.

This, for the solemn, the conventional, Wordsworth is pretty good going; and might make us wonder whether we have not overmuch subdued that violent young poet who wrote 'we murder to dissect'. But it fits in very well with the continual use of the word 'power'. It is in that power which is poetry that 'darkness makes abode'; it is in poetry that 'forms and substances'

> through the turnings intricate of verse
> Present themselves as objects recognized,
> In flashes, and with glory not their own.

In the first version he had written 'scarce their

own'; he gave to poetry in the last version a complete dominion. 'Woods and rills', 'fountains, meadows, hills and groves', are not to speak to us in poetry with their own authority. Wordsworth in fact was not ever writing a child's primer of Nature-mysticism; he left that to his commentators. He was himself concerned with the Nature 'that exists in works of mighty poets', with glory not its own.

It is then to such a future that the baby (already

> powerful in all sentiments of grief
> Of exultation, fear and joy)

is introduced. In certain fortunate cases, in the poets, this 'sensibility' is augmented and sustained, and the two great fostering virtues are 'beauty and fear'. These two themes run all through the *Prelude*, though for beauty is more often substituted the word joy. But it is a joy which is caused by beauty. And fear is, in Wordsworth, an emotion absolutely necessary to the poet's development: he stresses it continually. When he is speaking of the modern child, whom he did not like, he complains that

> natural or supernatural fear,
> Unless it leap upon him in a dream,
> Touches him not.

It is not a mere physical fear; it is indeed something which precludes this lesser terror. The example which he gives is his own experience, at the age of eight, when he saw the body of a dead man drawn up from Esthwaite Lake, 'a spectre shape Of terror'. But he, whose 'inner eye' had often seen such things before, in fairy-tales and romances, was unsubdued, and beheld it patterned and harmonized, decorated with 'ideal grace', and dignified as if already in poetry.

The kind of fear which he believed the young mind ought to undergo, and from which he thought modern education was separating it by over-anxious vigilance, protection, and instruction, is described in the two most famous passages of the First Book. The one tells how, after he had stolen a trapped bird from some one else's snare, he heard

> Low breathings coming after me, and sounds
> Of undistinguishable motion, steps
> Almost as silent as the turf they trod.

The second is when he had (again!) stolen some one else's boat, rowed out on the lake, and seen the huge peak, 'as if with voluntary power instinct'.

> After I had seen
> That spectacle, for many days, my brain
> Worked with a dim and undetermined sense
> Of unknown modes of being; o'er my thoughts
> There hung a darkness, call it solitude
> Or blank desertion. No familiar shapes
> Remained, no pleasant images of trees,
> Of sea or sky, no colours of green fields;
> But huge and mighty forms, that do not live
> Like living men, moved slowly through the mind
> By day, and were a trouble to my dreams.

The second passage is an enlargement of the first, and they are both great poetry. The poetic mind is aware of 'low breathings', 'sounds of undistinguishable motion', 'unknown modes of being', 'huge and mighty forms'. It is the pressure of the genius on the outer consciousness; this also perhaps is common to men.

But the poets are not content to leave it at that, as the rest of us largely have to do. An undetermined sense of unknown modes of being may be with them at their commencement, as with all of us. The difference in our developments is between those who lose that sense altogether (this is probably what is called 'losing one's early illusions'), those who keep it but cannot of themselves deal with it (among these are perhaps most of the readers of poetry), and those who are able to do something about it—and these are the poets. For their business is to discover and express, more and more exactly, more and more powerfully, those unknown modes of being. They work towards 'the two great ends of Liberty and Power'. Between those two passages are lines which may well have a secondary relation to the growing poetic genius.

> Dust as we are, the immortal spirit grows
> Like harmony in music; there is a dark
> Inscrutable workmanship that reconciles
> Discordant elements, makes them cling together
> In one society.

This is precisely the achievement of the great poets; in each of them discordant elements are united in one society by the inscrutable workmanship of their genius, and the society is the style.

But in the earlier period this unison is not yet consciously present. All things have the character 'of danger or desire'.

> The surface of the universal earth
> With triumph and delight, with hope and fear,

works 'like a sea'. For Wordsworth it was 'the

Presence of Nature' which brought this about, but it need not be only his kind of Nature to which such a disturbance is due; cities and men may produce it also.

There ensues on this a kind of personal determination by the poet. He encourages himself; he subjects himself at every opportunity to the experiences in which he discerns this power; in effect, he takes care that his soul 'is unsubdued' by the world. Wordsworth described himself as becoming attentive to the details of the things he observed, their 'transitory qualities'. But also he breathed in moods 'by form Or image unprofaned', moods in which 'visionary power' came to him. Visionary power here is identified with 'shadowy exultation'. Such moods are of use to the soul—to the poetic genius—because the memories of them teach it *how* it felt; they provide it with a sense of possible sublimity

whereto
With growing faculties she doth aspire,
With faculties still growing, feeling still
That whatsoever point they gain, they yet
Have something to pursue.

This is the labour of poetry; this is the very sense which attends on the writing of poetry. This 'something to pursue' is the something which lures and provokes the great poets into their greatness. The 'sublimity' of their experiences is the height to which they desire their analysing and synthesizing poetry to reach, and the infinite by which they measure their achievements.

But the poetic sense is still very much under the domination of the poet's personal enjoyments. The subjects of his contemplation receive part of their effect from his own mind. Wordsworth says

> What I saw
> Appeared like something in myself, a dream,
> A prospect in the mind.

The mind in fact imposes its own enjoyment on outer things; the sun, the birds, the wind, the fountain, the storm, appeared much more like themselves because Wordsworth willed them to be, and he derived increased transport from this knowledge. He coerced 'all things into sympathy'. Unless, intoxicated by his own feelings, he could feel 'the sentiment of Being spread o'er all', he was not perfectly contented. The young romantic poet, the young and violent Wordsworth, insisted on sending 'the fleshly ear' to sleep. It was natural; it was romantic. Even Milton had his *L'Allegro* and *Il Penseroso*—and everything in each of those great poetic gardens was lovely.

In the Third Book this process continues. The poetic mind is still imposing its own world on the world.

> I had a world about me—'twas my own;
> I made it, for it only lived to me,
> And to the God who sees into the heart.

But with this imposed unity went a no less strong sense of observed diversity. The strongest workings of his genius at that time were 'searching out the lines of difference'. It is at this point that Wordsworth exclaims in awe at the youthful might of 'souls'. He again attributes this power to every man: all do things 'within themselves' while earth is new. This is the 'genuine prowess' communicated from the point within the mind where each is single, from the poetic centre.

Nevertheless, in the new world of Cambridge this imagination for a while rests, except in its concern with mythology. It seeks the apprehension of antiquity and the powers of antiquity— Newton, Chaucer, Spenser, Milton; and by a natural but regrettable transition Wordsworth for some time leaves off talking of the creative soul and goes on to talk of William Wordsworth, Universities, Presidents, and Deans. It is not till he (symbolically) returns to 'his native hills' that he begins again to be interesting. The Fourth Book contains the famous dedication episode, but it is led up to by a warning of a change in apprehension. Something opens which Wordsworth calls ' human-heartedness '. Objects which have hitherto been 'the absolute wealth of his own private being' now cause other thoughts 'of change, congratulation, or regret'. Poetry is feeling the first faint stirrings of universal mortality as opposed to the attributed universalism of the poet's young emotions. The order of progress, he tells us, was from fear to delight and hope ('love enthusiastic'), and thence to this new thing. Poetry is beginning to write more about things, and less about what the poet felt about things.

Here Wordsworth knew of a difficulty which he was honest enough to admit. It would have been better to concentrate on solitary study, meditative peace. He *ought* to have done this. Yes, only— only the sense of his real dedication came to him *not* at such a concentration, but after a night of music and dancing and laughter and 'shocks of young love-liking'—presumably with the 'frank-hearted maids of rocky Cumberland'. Shakespeare perhaps would not have been surprised.

Book VI (*Cambridge and the Alps*) underlines another state of young genius. He is now dedicated; the poetic genius is conscious of its capacity, and looking forward (as Milton did) to doing lasting work. He is aware (i) of the more fanciful side of poetry, Spenserian visions; but also he is concerned with (2) abstractions—especially geometric; and (3) with indulgent moods of sadness. There is emphasized a consciousness of the difference between the youthful poetic apprehension and the mature. Even geometry is still 'a toy To sense embodied'; it is not yet a world 'created out of pure intelligence'. When, writing the *Prelude*, he looked back, he was conscious of his idleness at that time; perhaps because he was aware of the greater poetic material he might then have gathered. But he could not regret it, for all this time poetry itself was collecting itself in increasing power. It is still in an 'unripe state of intellect and heart', and later on (in Book VIII) we are told how Wordsworth always, at this time, attempted to decorate mere facts: an elder-tree growing by a mortuary must have a dismal look; a yew must have a ghost by it; a widow who has once visited the grave of her husband must do it every night.—'Dejection taken up for pleasure's sake' is a line which might describe her as well as Wordsworth. But the best description of the poet approaching poetry, of the great poet at work, occurs in those noble lines (VI. 592–616) which follow the crossing of the Alps.

Their immediate application is to Wordsworth's consciousness of the nature of man. But their secondary application is only less important.

> Imagination—here the Power so called
> Through sad incompetence of human speech,
> That awful Power rose from the mind's abyss
> Like an unfathered vapour that enwraps,
> At once, some lonely traveller. I was lost;
> Halted without an effort to break through;
> But to my conscious soul I now can say—
> 'I recognise thy glory:' in such strength
> Of usurpation, when the light of sense
> Goes out, but with a flash that has revealed
> The invisible world, doth greatness make abode,
> There harbours; whether we be young or old,
> Our destiny, our being's heart and home,
> Is with infinitude, and only there;
> With hope it is, hope that can never die,
> Effort, and expectation, and desire,
> And something evermore about to be.
> Under such banners militant, the soul
> Seeks for no trophies, struggles for no spoils
> That may attest her prowess, blest in thoughts
> That are their own perfection and reward,
> Strong in herself and in beatitude
> That hides her.

Any one who has ever written verse, will recognise the justice of

> hope that can never die,
> Effort, and expectation, and desire,
> And something evermore about to be.

The difference between the satisfactory and the unsatisfactory poet is in the last line. The good poet has patience and power to wait till that 'something about to be' has been brought about, however many minutes, hours, or years he may spend in effort and expectation and desire. Unsatisfactory poetry happens when, through incapacity or ignorance or impatience or poverty or kindness to others, the poet is content to write something down before the extreme moment of expectation has been reached, before the line has formed itself. That formation comes in a state in which the thought of spoils and prowess, of reward or fame, is equally blotted out, for nothing but poetry matters. In the great poets it is probably true—for Wordsworth said so—that the coming of the 'perfection and reward' is beatitude.

But also this passage is significant of the difference between the false imagination of the monotonous nightly visits of the widow to the yew, and the true imagination of sorrow, the difference between 'all the sad etcetera of the wrong' and the knowledge of the

> impersonated thought,
> The idea, or abstraction of this kind.

This consciousness of poetry—of imagination—breaks out again later, as he enters London on the top of a stage-coach. 'A weight of ages' descends on him—'weight and power'—'power growing under weight'. He spoke of Imagination as 'the Power so-called', and in London he continues to feel it thus. London provides him with 'strong sensations' of past and present; and he is craving for the power which such sensations provide. 'Influxes of power' come to him.

At the conclusion of the first part of the *Prelude*
then we have the poet intensely aware of the presence
of this power. The unknown modes of being—of
which he had been aware years before—are beginning
to shape themselves. All that he saw while he was
in London moved him passionately, but not beyond
the suburbs of the mind; the distinction is Wordsworth's, and he goes on to compare this movement
with the movement of which he was conscious after
he had been reading Shakespeare (VII. 477–85).

> realities of act and mien,
> The incarnation of the spirits that move
> In harmony amid the Poet's world,
> Rose to ideal grandeur, or, called forth
> By power of contrast, made me recognise,
> As at a glance, the things which I had shaped,
> And yet not shaped, had seen and scarcely seen,
> When, having closed the mighty Shakspeare's page,
> I mused, and thought, and felt, in solitude.

It seems that Shakespeare's poetry was still
affecting him rather as that mountain of his youth
had done; he was left with 'an undetermined sense',
and yet sufficiently determined to enable him to
recognise 'realities of act and mien', the 'incarnation
of the spirits that' moved, necessarily, in his own
world of poetry. His genius was recognising its
own power. He gives one example—that of a blind
beggar wearing a placard describing his story;
Wordsworth saw it as if that scrawled label was all
that we could know of ourselves and the universe—
the beggar loomed on him, a supernatural apparition,
one of those mysterious solitaries who crossed and
recrossed his own solitary and awful path.

Poetry is on the very verge of greatness. The poet is aware both of the diversity and unity of things. He feels, and he knows he feels, the power of Imagination moving within him.

This is the end of the Seventh Book; the Eighth is Retrospect. The Ninth opens with quite a different note, and so far as poets in general are concerned, the rest of the tale is short—'Oh, how much unlike the past!'

Every one knows it. The Revolution broke out and all emotions and thoughts were swept into a unity of delight and wonder. The unknown modes of being were taking on the shape of a renewed world. Wordsworth himself did not much feel this new world in the abstract idea of freedom—he tells us how he picked up a stone from the ruins of the Bastille, 'affecting more emotion than I felt'. But this was a part of a danger he notes several times, the tendency to provoke the false emotion instead of the real, the lingering habit of encouraging the widow to come every night. The poet experiences 'real fervour', but also that 'less genuine and wrought up within myself'. It is when he sees men and women —the 'hunger-bitten girl', Beaupuy, and the people,

> from the depth
> Of shameful imbecility uprisen,

that his spirit is really stirred.

> Bliss was it in that dawn to be alive,
> But to be young was very heaven.

Power from the mountains and lakes of West-morland, from London strangers, from Shake-

speare; power from the Revolution, from the work
of honour France was doing—

> from all doubt
> Or trepidation for the end of things
> Far was I, far as angels are from guilt.

There was no doubt; there might be distress,
but the great movement accordant with all his past
prophesied its august end. And then the English
Government declared war on the Revolution.

Wordsworth, in his account of the matter, has
been blamed for admitting, in the later version of
the *Prelude*, a little gush of patriotism just previous
to his account of this crisis. It is not very good
poetry certainly, but Wordsworth may have had a
reason for letting it in. He may have wished to
accentuate the fact that he had a quick sense of
England as well as of France. He did feel that the
'sacred ground' of 'Albion' had given way under
him; the mountains of England were at war with
the plains of France, and he was ravaged by the fact
of that conflict. Change, injustice, evil, could then
be.

> Not in my single self alone I found,
> But in the minds of all ingenuous youth,
> Change and subversion from that hour. No shock
> Given to my moral nature had I known
> Down to that very moment; neither lapse
> Nor turn of sentiment that might be named
> A revolution, save at this one time;
> All else was progress on the self-same path
> On which, with a diversity of pace,
> I had been travelling: this a stride at once
> Into another region.

There fell upon him 'a conflict of sensations without name'. Things were changed 'into their contraries'. In the poets, the poetic mind is the most intense and enduring thing for good or evil, and they must feel such a conflict, such a revolution and subversion, in their genius. That genius is their soul; the wound is dealt to their soul. Wordsworth was wounded there, and never recovered. It is not the smallest count against the government of England of that day. 'Power' had been within him; it was changed into its contrary. There was with him in his dreams

> a sense
> Death-like, of treacherous desertion, felt
> In the last place of refuge—my own soul.

From the point of view of poetry there are no more important lines in the *Prelude*, and few as important. For the result of that desertion is given later:

> The days gone by
> Return upon me almost from the dawn
> Of life; the hiding-places of man's power
> Open; I would approach them, but they close.

In those lines Wordsworth, ostensibly looking back towards his childhood and seeking to recall the moments by which his mind had been 'nourished and invisibly repaired', did more than that. He recalls —to the submissive reader, if not to himself—the 'unknown modes of being'; he asserts what his genius meant, and was meant, to do; he declares the failure of his genius to do it. Wordsworth is our third greatest poet, but even Wordsworth was never the poet he should have been. It is with a sense of

profound irony that the reader finds him speaking
of the dream which

> entangled me
> In long orations, which I strove to plead
> Before unjust tribunals.

The dream did but prophesy his doom; from then
till now much of Wordsworth's verse has been
regarded precisely as his genius entangled in long
orations before our unjust tribunals. Unjust, at
least, if there is the smallest kind of patronage. It
is not merely iniquitous, it is imbecile, to patronize
Wordsworth—only a little more iniquitous and imbecile than to patronize Coleridge; it is cutting our
initials in Westminster Abbey or the Parthenon. It
will be time enough to patronize or pardon the great
ones when we can also do things that are 'felt in the
blood and felt along the heart'.

This was Wordsworth's personal experience. But
that is not the immediate point. An experience *of
that kind* is here the subject of the poetry—it happens
to be his own, which is interesting to the biographer
but unimportant for poetry. His poetry is here
concerned to discover, to express, to define, a particular state of being. We are no longer in the presence
of low breathings and silent steps; nor even of some
huge and mighty form that is a trouble to our dreams.
On the contrary we are shown a form which is a
trouble not to its own or our dreams, but to its own
and our life. Poetry is here awakening in us our
sense of our capacity for 'change and subversion'—
for 'a conflict of sensations without name'. Wordsworth happens to be the writer of the verse, but the
Wordsworth who is the subject is that almost

mythical figure who sits in the village church, silent, revengeful, solitary; the figure whose soul is only aware of a mystical desertion, the figure thrown 'out of the pale of love'.

The *Prelude* is an account of Wordsworth's mind up to the writing of *Lyrical Ballads*. But it is something else too; it is an account of the developing powers of poetry up to the time when poetry imagines to itself a crisis of utter overthrow and desolation. At the beginning of the work of all the poets is an undetermined sense of unknown modes of being; the aim of all poets is to approach the hiding-places of man's power, to discover the impersonated thought. Even of the poets there have not been many who do this; Wordsworth himself did so only in a limited sense. The remainder of the *Prelude* does not carry the history of the poetic mind in general much farther, though it is full of illuminating phrases on poetry, and though it tells us of the immediate future of Wordsworth's own mind. But in doing so it continually looks back; it recovers sight of its awful sources but hardly contact with them. The close of the *Prelude* is one of the noblest passages in English verse. But the subject of that close is the poet doing something; it awakens our capacity to learn, to believe, to know. Wordsworth promises to indoctrinate us; his poetry, rising to a marvellous lucidity, flashes on us the consciousness of the mind of man

> above this frame of things . . .
> In beauty exalted, as it is itself
> Of quality and fabric more divine.

'Clear as crystal . . . descending out of heaven', wrote another poet. It is poetry declaring its own salvation.

But Wordsworth's personal intention was to instruct man; he is concerned more with our belief than with that divine fabric.

But before considering Wordsworth's own achievement it will be more convenient to see what other parallels to that 'change and subversion' exist in English verse.

III

THE CYCLE OF SHAKESPEARE

I

SHAKESPEARE has said very little about the function of a poet or about the life of genius. But the volume of the plays is in itself, if not an exposition of the one, at least an example of the other. The authority of a major scholar and of a major poet, Sir Edmund Chambers and Mr. Lascelles Abercrombie, is sufficient to justify lesser minds in accepting that volume, roughly, as canonical: certainly for the purpose for which it will be used here.

That purpose is to consider the changes in Shakespeare's way of dealing with things in his poetry. It involves no thesis about his nature except that he was a poet, nor about his life except that he made a (prosperous) living by writing plays. He may have been a neurotic or a philosopher, a commercial magnate or a spiritual ascetic, a tender friend or a Christian Shylock. Or all at once. He may even have been Bacon, or Oxford, or Burleigh, or Queen Elizabeth, or Archbishop Whitgift—we are concerned only with the poetry, by whomsoever it was written. Interestingly enough, this poetry is to be found in the poetry, not in anything else.[1]

---

[1] I have not been anxious to compel myself to mention every play; the danger of ingenuity is too great. And though any new and certain discovery about dates might mean a re-telling of this tale, it could not wholly destroy it. *The Tempest* is not likely to be found to be earlier than the *Two Gentlemen*, nor *Antony* a trial-essay towards

Every poet, like every man, sets out to enjoy himself. The English Muse, defeated so many times in this early occupation with 'life, liberty, and the pursuit of happiness', seems to renew her search with undiminished ardour at every opportunity. Even Milton was not born old; even Mr. Housman has written happy lyrics. Hardy certainly—but some of even Hardy's early inventions had a certain grotesquerie about them, as if his genius were playing a little with the bones of men. No one can take 'thy worm shall be my worm, love' quite seriously. It is a wan, a very romantic, hope; but it is a hope, and a deliberate enjoyment. Of this early delight Shakespeare had his full share. The diction of the plays is part of it: consider the dance of words, the puns and the rhymes, for instance in the antiphon between Luciana and Antipholus in the *Comedy of Errors*.

And more even than in the diction this enjoyment is felt in the manner of emotional apprehension. The bodies in *Titus Andronicus*, the proclaimed villainy of Richard III, the reckless and unconvincing pardon of Proteus in *Two Gentlemen*, are all examples of Shakespeare 'having a good time'. Perhaps *Romeo and Juliet* contains the best example of all; hardly anywhere else has death, while remaining sad, been made more purely luxurious than in Romeo's great speech, and this speech is in accord with the play. There is no malice and no injustice, except by chance. Quarrels do break out; letters

Troilus. The Clarendon Press have allowed me to reproduce in an appendix to this book Sir Edmund Chambers's tentative chronology of the plays.

do go wrong; appointments are missed; and death
happens. What can one do about it? Nothing but
enjoy.

In each of the earlier romantic comedies there is,
speaking generally, a broad division—there is the
poetic part and the comic part. These are sometimes
held together by the plot; sometimes they are
separate. Launce and Speed in the *Two Gentlemen*
have nothing to do with the plot, the Dromios in
the *Comedy of Errors* are closer; in *Love's Labour's
Lost* the comic characters are brought under the
same law without any serious connexion with the
others; in the *Midsummer-Night's Dream* the two
groups are more closely intertwined. The *Taming
of the Shrew* is all comic and little romantic manage-
ment. But comic or romantic, the same characteristics mark each play and each division in the play—
there is dance-music in them all, now verbal, now
personal: they are willing to pretend—from the
two pairs of twins in the *Comedy of Errors* to the three
caskets and the bond in the *Merchant of Venice*. In
the plays of 1592–4 we have, on the one hand, the
gorgeous pretence of melodrama: the murders in
Richard III and the murders in *Andronicus* are almost
the height of a young man enjoying bloody violence
for the sake of bloody violence; just as, on the other
hand, in the *Errors* and in the *Shrew* a riotous good-
tempered violence is called in to resolve the dance of
misunderstanding and opposition. Daggers or sticks
are the solvers of all crises. Something of this comic
dance Shakespeare retained till very late: if the
gravediggers in *Hamlet* could ever be persuaded to
abandon their realism and be quicker at their talk

than they are at their job, if they could play their play as if they were a comic chorus rather than navvies from London streets, we might be more amused at them.

But the 'hero' also appears thus early. *Richard III* depends on the personal effectiveness of Richard; the *Shrew* on the personal effectiveness of Petruchio. Action, tyrannical action (if we may abolish morality for a moment), broad tyrannical action, is their occupation and characteristic: from this seed the discoveries of Shakespeare sprang. His genius seems to say, almost in so many words, that when it did not choose to

> prove a lover
> To entertain these fair well-spoken days,
> [It was] determinèd to prove a villain
> And hate the idle pleasures of these days.

Even Richard III—Renaissance prince as he was —probably never actually sang himself so responsively into the throne.

The riotous battles of those early plays are intellectualized in *Love's Labour's Lost*. The young laughter of Shakespeare's poetry there becomes a part of the poetry; the verse indulges itself with a romantic idea and with romantic laughter at the romantic idea. The comic side is intellectualized also; everything is to be kept in the same courtly key—no doubt because it was for a courtly entertainment. But that is only the motive and opportunity, not the act and the poetry. Battle had been noisy; it is now exquisite. But it still exists, between the King and his courtiers and the Princess and her ladies; between the individual lovers; between Armado and

Costard; between culture and pedantry; between the men's intentions and their actions; between—how lightly! how joyously! but still between—intention and necessity. There was to be another play of opposition, made up of oppositions, another play of love's labour, long afterwards, but that would be called not, as this might be, *Berowne and Rosaline* but *Antony and Cleopatra*. It was not then to be the exquisiteness of the pattern which caused delight, nor was death to be introduced far off merely to end a play. And in some sense—again ever so lightly— Berowne's line breathes a coming change.

'Worthies, away! the scene begins to cloud.' It is not only in the lovely seriousness of the conclusion; it is more clearly in the accompanying plays—in *Romeo and Juliet*, in *Richard II*, in *A Midsummer-Night's Dream* that the cloud appears—different in all, yet something the same in all. In *Romeo* its name is accident; in *Richard II*, Bolingbroke; in the *Dream*, Puck or Oberon or, perhaps even more exactly, 'a little western flower'. It cannot be called Fate, but it is something incalculable and sometimes destructive. It is not enough to make the poetry seriously attend to it; or rather—at least, in the two romantic plays—it only offers poetry an opportunity of dancing to new measures, of luxuriating in grief, of turning fairies into charming copies of men and women.[1]

Yet poetry is still in the stage that Wordsworth described when he spoke of 'unknown modes of being'. Romeo's great speech is precisely that.

[1] To look forward again—in precisely the opposite manner to that by which, in the *Tempest*, Shakespeare was to abandon mankind.

Shakespeare is thoroughly enjoying himself in luxurious grief. There is no analysis of many emotions; it is all magniloquence and brave rhetoric of sorrow. We know nothing more about Romeo at the end than at the beginning, nor do we want. It is perfect —for Romeo. With it may be compared the chorus that laments in the Capulets' house over Juliet; in the midst of which Shakespeare does not in the least mind having his little bit of fun with the Nurse— 'Death is my son-in-law; Death is my heir', says Capulet, and the Nurse almost parodies him, and then Paris elegantly paraphrases her, and then Capulet comes back. It is, no doubt, partly the fashion of speech and behaviour of the time. Capulet might, in Elizabethan London, have said just that: 'Death is my son-in-law; Death is my heir'. But Shakespeare did not risk having any one like the Nurse about when he came to Constance—

> Grief fills the room up of my absent child,
> Lies in his bed, walks up and down with me,
> Puts on his pretty looks, repeats his words,
> Remembers me of all his gracious parts,
> Stuffs out his vacant garments with his form.

This is the banishment of Wordsworth's widow: the coming of 'a grave unto a soul'. Much more like it in *Romeo* is Mercutio's dying epigram, more incidental than Romeo's but more directly effective— 'No, 'tis not so deep as a well, nor so wide as a church door; but 'tis enough, 'twill serve.' It is a sharper prophecy of the realism that was to come than 'insubstantial death is amorous'. Or rather the two speeches are two sides of a single thing; the greater poetry was peeping out here and there through

chinks and crevices, lines and phrases. When it
fully emerged all the irony and truth of ''twill serve'
were found to be one with 'the palace of dim night'.
Romeo's speech and state of being is 'a palace of
dim night', a palace afterwards measured by phrases
and meanings as exact as 'deep as a well . . . wide as
a church door'.

But this is an appearance of material tragedy;
there exists also in the play—I think the first—
appearance of spiritual evil, in the unexpected and
sudden apostasy of the Nurse, who has her moment
and becomes a premonition of horror. Juliet has
defied her father and mother, refusing to marry Paris,
in a strenuous devotion to romantic love. When
they go, she turns to the Nurse with an exquisite
phrase—

> What sayst thou? hast thou not a word of joy?
> Some comfort, Nurse?

The 'word of joy' which the Nurse offers is advice to
marry Paris—'Romeo's a dishclout to him', and

> is dead; or 'twere as good he were,
> As living here, and you no use of him.

'The use of him' that Juliet still has, the intense
imagination and sense of him that fills her, is understood at once, not merely now to be, but through all
the play to have been, entirely beyond the Nurse's
apprehension. Her good humour, her harmless
sensuality, is understood at once to be, in her case,
a greedy and acquiescent sensuality—the enemy, not
the ally, of 'true love's passion'. Love is to her but
a use of him, a convenience, a pleasure. It is with
the indignation of poetry itself that Juliet breathes

after her (her back, as she hobbles away, turned on that high imagination which Juliet's love possesses), breathes after the denial of poetry itself—

Ancient damnation! O most wicked fiend!

It is not merely that the Nurse is a realist; Falstaff is a realist. But if Falstaff had ever wanted to give similar advice, he would have done it by defeating imagination by imagination; he would have cast out one spirit by another. The Nurse is thinking of casting out spirit by flesh.

To mention Falstaff is to enter on another stage of Shakespeare's imagination. But before Falstaff there is in *King John* a figure who possesses a unity which was afterwards to be divided, the significant figure of the Bastard. The poetry which the Bastard speaks is of various kinds marvellously harmonized. He is ironical and realistic, passionate and faithful, patriotic and pitiful. Even Henry V does not greatly improve on his warlike rhetoric; even Kent in *Lear* hardly more definitely, though perhaps more profoundly, conveys a sense of solitary devotion to his sovereign; even Falstaff or Hamlet need not have been ashamed of the sense of the speech on Commodity, though their style might have been more intense; even in *Macbeth* there is hardly a more real, though there is a vaster and more awful, sense of tragic murder than in his utterances to Hubert after the death of Arthur. Shakespeare's poetry began to say, with him,

I am amazed, methinks, and lose my way
Among the thorns and dangers of this world.

It was not true of Faulconbridge; it was not to be

true of the poetry. But it is true that Faulconbridge is the last completely balanced figure for some time —certainly among all the plays of active business, the historical plays, and even perhaps until Imogen. He is not master of the profoundest poetry. But that is because Shakespeare's genius was not yet capable of giving it to him. He is the last character of whom we feel not only the possibility that in any exterior or interior crises he would 'keep his head', but also that he is capable of interior crises. He is not so great a figure as Falstaff, nor so blazing a figure as Henry V. But he could meet either of them on almost equal terms. He is, so to speak, the ideal ordinary man, and, being that, he is the problem which Shakespeare had to solve, and the material to solve it. The last few lines are certainly a patriotic conclusion to a patriotic play; but they are also a self-possessed conclusion to a self-possessed character. 'We do them wrong'—at least we do their poetry wrong, to extract them in anthologies; for they are the Bastard's patriotism, not ours, and they are only properly spoken when they are spoken by him. It is his trueness to himself which enables him to say so convincingly

> Naught shall make us rue
> If England to itself do rest but true.

He is proportioned in the adequacy of his emotions and his intelligence; he is rightly adequate, and it was on this theme of adequacy that Shakespeare provided us with his great variations—Bottom, Falstaff, Henry V: all more developed characters than the Bastard, yet every one lacking something of his completeness. Bottom is more unconscious, Falstaff is more self-conscious, Henry is more professionally, more purposefully, conscious. 'The thorns and dangers of this world' were trodden down in different ways by all of them. But not a single one of them would have been capable of saying those two lines with that intonation of intelligence, humility, courage, and simplicity. Some singleness was done and left when Shakespeare went three ways at once into the Bastard's totality.

Bottom was the first. *Richard II* and the *Dream* are both full of the same luxuriating delight which *Romeo* had: only in one play it was mostly concentred in the King, and in the other Shakespeare retains it himself and lavishes it everywhere. The King is opposed by Bolingbroke. But in the *Dream*, the court, the lovers, the fairies, are all ranged opposite Bottom. These two kinds of figures remained through several plays Shakespeare's chief concern in character until gradually the sufficient figure stood alone. One way or another, the Bastard, Bottom, Falstaff, Henry V, are persons complete in themselves, self-sufficient, victorious over their worlds. The style of verse (where verse is used) alters to express them; it loses its luxury, it lives in the enjoyment of direct movement. Bottom and Falstaff are given chiefly prose to speak: their self-imaginations, their outward or inward contemplations, would have delayed the active verse too long. Not till *Julius Caesar* did interior contemplation and movement come together again.

Petruchio had been adequate to the crisis which was Katherine. He had been personally effective.

But Bottom is adequate to any crisis, through a much
larger personal effectiveness. He and Falstaff are
opposites and complements; they attain similar
triumphs by contrasted qualities. Bottom is never
conscious of himself; Falstaff always is. Bottom
gets his own way everywhere by virtue of that
enormous simplicity which he carries like a great
gold bludgeon. But Falstaff overrules every situation
—except one—by descending on and all over it
not merely in a shower of gold but in a shower of
minted gold. Confronted with any situation Bottom
knocks it down—'I will walk . . . I will sing', 'Nay,
I can gleek', 'I will sing it before the Duke'. He
knocks down the actors by his commands; when
Theseus makes a rash remark he is immediately
knocked down by an explanation. Oberon and
Titania (it is pleasant to think) escape from him while
he is asleep. But if neither Titania nor Theseus nor
his own neighbours, nor an ass's head nor his own
head, can abash a man, what is there in a just
universe which can? And that the universe is just
—or rather, that it is not unjust, not malicious or
cruel—is a fundamental assumption in comedy.
We must either believe that, or forget that we believe
the opposite. More—it must be courteous; it must
be willing to waive its strict rights. Justice perhaps
demands that you shall not be cheated. But if you
know you are being cheated, and enjoy the beauty
of the cheating, and prefer so to be cheated, it
would be a boorish universe that would intrude.
It is just, but that justice takes account of our own
wishes and enjoyments. The grudge we have against
Shakespeare is that, having educated us to enjoy

being cheated by Falstaff, he then insists that we must not be allowed to enjoy it. He does it in a sentence—'Let us take any man's horses; the laws of England are at my commandment.' Yes—this will never do; we must rebuke and chastise Falstaff. But we have shared in the fault; the laws of England have been broken for our delight when we sat in the Justice's court and heard the pressing and the bribing or were at the cozening of Mistress Quickly. It is not the Prince who behaves badly to Falstaff—he at least has meant to do nothing else all along and Shakespeare with him; it is we who have betrayed him because of our own respectability.

But Falstaff was probably never friends with us, whatever we thought. He uses his wit, as his courage, proportionally to the need. He plays with the Prince; he plays—more warily and more distantly—with the Chief Justice; he tires of John of Lancaster after two or three speeches and lets him go.

> Fare you well, Falstaff, I in my condition
> Shall better speak of you than you deserve.

'I would you had but the wit; 'twere better than your dukedom.' He will spend as perfect a thought on his Page—'I do here walk before thee like a sow that hath overwhelmed all her litter but one.' But when it came to showing this enormous power 'in love', Shakespeare did not choose to do it, for part of Falstaff's greatness is that he realizes that he himself is too vast to spend on others. But our imagination of love—however action falls short—is that ourself should be spent on some other. The pouring out of this large self-sufficiency on another—its knowledge

THE CYCLE OF SHAKESPEARE

of humility, of tenderness, of shyness—would have asked all Shakespeare's power, and if the *Merry Wives* was roughly contemporaneous with *Hamlet*, Shakespeare was then engaged, as we shall see, on quite another business. At the point of *Henry IV*, however, Falstaff is the great comic figure, content to know himself with as little action as need be. He is the impersonation of the comic idea in the world. 'The brain of this foolish-compounded clay, man, is not able to invent anything that tends to laughter more than I invent or is invented on me; I am not only witty in myself, but the cause that wit is in other men.'

The Epilogue to 2 *Henry IV* promises *Henry V* 'with Sir John in it', though 'for anything I know, Falstaff shall die of a sweat' in France. He did die, and for at least one simple reason, that even Shakespeare would not, or could not, then include two separate and vital spiritual universes in one play. His own mind obviously was capable of intensely appreciating both, but there was no way of uniting them. For the contradiction between them to be exhibited in Shakespeare's style it would have to be done by a vivid personal experience. Such a contradiction, though of another kind, his poetry was to find out later: at present he had two 'philosophical' principles, each 'an idea, or abstraction of its kind', exposed to view each as an element in a particular living person.

Henry, in one of his most famous speeches, stresses one.

> But if it be a sin to covet honour
> I am the most offending soul alive. . . .

God's peace! I would not lose so great an honour
As one man more, methinks, would share from me,
For the best hope I have.

All the play ardently supports him—'honour's
thought', 'Dishonour not your mothers', 'O! for
honour of our land', 'By faith and honour', 'spirit of
honour', 'but that our honours must not', 'the fewer
men the greater share of honour', 'draw their honours
reeking up to heaven', 'let's die in honour', 'his
honour-owing wounds', 'an honourable badge', 'your
Grace does me as great honours', 'wear it for our
honour', 'from my weary limbs Honour is cudgell'd'.
Honour, doubtless in the interior, but even more in
the exterior, sense, is the subject, and it has glory for
an aureole. Henry himself had been talking in this
strain as far back as 1 *Henry IV*, when he engaged
himself to pluck Hotspur's honours from him.
Another voice however sounded then.

Well, 'tis no matter; honour pricks me on. Yea, but
how if honour prick me off when I come on? how then?
Can honour set to a leg? No. Or an arm? No. Or take
away the grief of a wound? No. Honour hath no skill in
surgery then? No. What is honour? a word. What is that
word, honour? Air. A trim reckoning! Who hath it? he that
died o' Wednesday. Doth he feel it? No. Doth he hear it?
No. It is insensible then? Yea, to the dead. But will it not
live with the living? No. Why? Detraction will not suffer
it. Therefore I'll none of it: honour is a mere scutcheon;
and so ends my catechism.

If Falstaff had been Parolles this might not have
mattered. But Falstaff is very much not Parolles.
Sir John Coleville is introduced in 2 *Henry IV*

apparently merely to surrender to him—as if Shakespeare were a little afraid that even his having led his 'ragamuffins where they are peppered' might not have made us forget the early running-away. But it did not need. Falstaff has a realistic sense of proportion, and was the least likely man in the world to run a risk of death in a night robbery. Poins knew it—'if he fight longer than he see reason'. A brave man, who not only has no passion for honour or glory, but who is capable of abolishing the whole universe in which such things exist by a few phrases, is no character for *Henry V*. It is not that Henry is less convincing; it is that no reader or spectator can be convinced both by Henry and Falstaff on this subject in the same play. What would Westmoreland have done if Falstaff had had a chance at him? Something of the same challenge, but reversed, occurs later in the answer of Sir Toby Belch to Malvolio —'Dost thou think, because thou art virtuous, there shall be no more cakes and ale?' Something of the same dispute was attempted, but in a very different way, in the great scene between Claudio and Isabella in *Measure for Measure*: Isabella's honour against Claudio's life: two 'impersonated thoughts' meeting. But that kind of philosophic discussion and decision was not to be Shakespeare's method; it was abandoned, as we shall see, once for all, in *Troilus*.

Yet it might be thought, at the end of *Henry V*, that Shakespeare would have to return on his steps. He had followed one road to Falstaff, and what more could be done for adequacy? He had followed another road to Henry V, and what more could be done for adequacy? *Henry V* might have been a conclusion; it is only a pause.

The speech of Henry's before Agincourt, and indeed his whole behaviour, but especially that single speech, has the final unity of the active life; the phrase 'brothers in arms' is ennobled and exalted in it. All the subtlety of the outer world is in it. It arouses our capacity of understanding fellowship, a fellowship of preparation for, and contempt of, death. The ardent purpose of communal life in a world of activity and danger overrides the prospect of death. As far as can be in that world the idea of death is conquered. 'Victory or Westminster Abbey'—man and the honour of man find in the plangent exterior life no more glorious or more fitting climax.

But that swift, lucid, effective verse stayed, and changed. The style had so far been romantic or comic or historic. But the romantic (even in *Richard II*) had been enjoying itself; and the comic had assumed—as comedy always must, either as a fact or a pretence—that the universe was just; and the historic had been patriotically honourable, and honourably patriotic. But if sorrow—not merely, as with Constance, for a few moments, but for whole plays—left off enjoying itself? and if deliberate injustice came in? and if the historic lost its patriotism? It was about this time that *Twelfth Night* and *Julius Caesar* were written. *Twelfth Night* is the opposite of Falstaff. *Julius Caesar* is the alteration of Henry V. And both are the progress to *Hamlet*.

II

If *Much Ado* came in 1598–9, just about the time of *Henry V*—perhaps before—and *Twelfth Night* in 1599–1600—perhaps just after *Julius Caesar*; if, that is, *Much Ado* came before *Twelfth Night*, then its extremely unsatisfactory nature is explained. It is an unconscious 'try-out' for the later play; it lies in the connexion of the *Comedy of Errors*, *Love's Labour's Lost*, the *Dream*, and *Twelfth Night*; and these are in a definite relation, even a progress. The progress is in the method—which is a more suitable word than to say subject; and the method is deception. Some kind of cheat takes place in all these plays— a cheat natural but not necessary to comedy. Some sort of cheat occurs in *Romeo*, the *Merchant*, and *As You Like It* also, but of an incidental kind. In the *Errors* the deception is almost mechanical: A is supposed to be A1, and A1 to be A. In *Love's Labour's Lost*, it is double—(1) the deception which the lords practise on each other, and on the Princess, (2) the deception which necessity practises on the lords. In the *Dream* it is enchantment, neither mechanical nor intellectual. In *Much Ado* it is, largely, a mess; a play in which a greater number of people were listening at keyholes or with less poetry Shakespeare never wrote. Benedick over-hears, Beatrice overhears, Claudio and Don Pedro overhear, the Watch overhear; a masked ball and a veiled bride complete what Shakespeare called a plot. *Much Ado about Nothing* is a profoundly significant title. It has of course its wit and its mild amusement; it has one magnificent moment—

Beatrice's 'Kill Claudio'. But in *Twelfth Night* Shakespeare did it all over again—only this time the deception was psychological—except for the dear old twins, but they are made lovely; and for the trick on Malvolio. Those two details, however, are not the main thing. Nevertheless, including them, consider the manner of the play, the maze of deception, done so easily that it is not always recognized. There is (1) Viola's deception of the Duke and (2) of Olivia; (3) Orsino's self-deception in his love; (4) Olivia's self-deception in her mourning; (5) Malvolio's self-deception; (6) the trick on Malvolio; (7) Aguecheek's half-deception by Sir Toby; (8) all the Sebastian episodes. Almost everybody—except perhaps Viola and Sir Toby—is gently mocked: but Orsino and Olivia most. This then is enduring love, enduring sorrow! the exact comment is made in that last song which is one of the greatest things in Shakespeare and in our literature.

> There is no woman's sides
> Can bide the beating of so strong a passion
> As love doth give my heart.

> *A great while ago the world began.*

> The element itself, till seven years' heat,
> Shall not behold her face at ample view;
> But, like a cloistress, she will veiled walk,
> And water once a day her chamber round
> With eye-offending brine.

> *By swaggering could I never thrive.*

She uses me with a more exalted respect than anyone else that follows her.

When that I was and a little tiny boy.

'Slid, I'll after him again and beat him.

With toss-pots still had drunken heads.

I'll be revenged on the whole pack of you.

A great while ago the world began.

It is a song of this play, and of all the plays up to the
agonies: the turning-point from the light to darkness,
and itself—could one bear it—a comment at once
on joy and grief. It is neither comic nor tragic nor
ironic, but rather poetry's own comment on all that
had hitherto been done. Nor over that play alone
does the song brood. It answers from a distance the
brave beauty of Agincourt; it is the only sound that
can meet Falstaff's phrases, though he is too much
a realist for it to mock him. It dims, as the mortals
they met could not, the bright fairies of the *Dream*,
and brings even the soliloquies of Richard II into
the daily rain, so that they trudge a little shiveringly.
One thing does not enter its simplicity and that is
death—for a song to speak of that with as single a
note as this of life we must wait for the dirge in
Cymbeline.

In *Henry V* Shakespeare had avoided opposition
and contradiction by killing Falstaff. In *Twelfth
Night* he brought opposition in and reconciled it by
invoking a delicate and joyous deception or self-
deception everywhere. In *Julius Caesar* for the first
time he allows the opposition which is in the nature
of things to run its course; the dream world of
Brutus is contrasted with the actual world of Caesar
and Caesar's ghost. And this world of Caesar's is so

actual that it can dominate even Caesar's own deaf-
ness, baldness, and falling-sickness. His magniloquent phrases are given all obstacles to their success
—even their own magniloquence—and overcome
them, 'Hence! wilt thou lift up Olympus?' What
absurd rant! only the play itself supports it—'O
Julius Caesar, thou art mighty yet.' It is a self-
deception; only in this case it is not a deception.
There is self-deception in the play, but it is not with
Caesar. It is with another character, a character
who perhaps suffers from it, for Shakespeare's genius
never quite 'finished off' Brutus. Or let us say that
it finished him off without being quite certain until
the very end in what that finishing off consisted.
Brutus is one of those characters—perhaps the only
character—in whom it might be argued that Shakespeare's touch is a little uncertain, not merely from
accident or carelessness, but because he really did
not quite know what he wanted to do. Either that
or else we must attribute to Shakespeare *at that
time* a profundity of poetic knowledge which the
phrases of the style hardly possess. Brutus is, in
effect, the passing of Shakespeare's concern from
sufficiency (as in Henry V) to insufficiency (as in
Hamlet).

Under the glorious golden figure of Henry looking out over the harbour of poetry—Southampton,
perhaps, where he 'embarked his royalty' for France
—the tides ebb out towards the wider seas. *Twelfth
Night* and *Julius Caesar* are the moaning of the bar
—beautiful or fearful. Something else is coming in;
in *Julius Caesar* the first of the unknown powers
which are Ghosts or Witches appears; powers not

entirely of the mind, for they reveal things which those who see them do not know; yet not entirely outside the mind, for those who see them recognize their messages quickly enough. The sound of the poetry changes. The infinity of Falstaff's prose had ceased before Henry's banners and trumpets, which accompanied 'his bruised helmet and his bended sword'. This valour had endured its own danger in the Chorus which is the vigil in the darkness before Agincourt. 'The royal captain of a ruined band' had finished with his crisis, and now another music breathed itself out, gently at first, as the tide against the shore, but afterwards to grow into the oceanic storms. I would almost go so far as to say that the dramatic apprehensiveness in *Julius Caesar* is a reflection of the poetic apprehensiveness which Shakespeare felt in himself. It is there; it is there because it is dramatically appropriate. But if it had to be there anyhow because it was in Shakespeare, that may explain why it was, as the play arranged itself, dramatically appropriate.

For the verse of the play is continually apprehensive. It is spoken by men who are always expecting; they are on the point of acting, or having acted they are uncertainly looking for a result. Or, consciously or unconsciously, they are on the point of suffering. There is uncertainty in Brutus and Cassius and all Rome whether Caesar will accept the crown; Cassius is uncertain—and Brutus is uncertain—what Brutus himself will do; the success of the conspiracy is uncertain—and when it has succeeded its result is uncertain, just as Caesar is uncertain whether or not to go to the Senate, just as Antony after the assassination is uncertain of his own fate, just as the conspirators are uncertain of the result of his speaking, just as the mob are uncertain of their real thoughts, or again the conspirators of the result of the last battle. The 'sway of earth Shakes like a thing infirm'. The friends part—'If we do meet again'—'O that a man might know!'

This recurrent doubt is accentuated by the continual disagreement between Brutus and Cassius. They are always disputing what they shall do. After Brutus has entered the conspiracy he overrules Cassius four separate times—apart from their quarrel —(1) in his refusal to admit Cicero, (2) in his refusal to kill Antony, (3) in giving Antony permission to speak, (4) in marching to Philippi. The last three decisions are fatal to the success of the conspirators. He has perfectly good reasons (in both senses of the word 'good'), only they always bring him into difficulty, and at last to death.

The failure of Brutus's reason is half the play. He and his friends are rational and uncertain; Caesar, alive or dead, is irrational and certain. He changes his mind again and again about going to the Senate, though he brags of being unchangeable. But, though this may be Shakespeare's deliberate irony, it remains true that there is in every change a complete assent; he alters but he does not vacillate. But in Brutus reason becomes more and more parted from himself until he throws it over altogether, abandons his philosophy, and accepts the thing which is beyond philosophy. There is the notorious scene in which, as we have it, he hears of his wife's death and then pretends he has not, in order to appear publicly as the Roman stoic. This is perhaps an accident of the text, like the double speech in *Love's Labour's Lost*. Perhaps, but not every one feels that such behaviour is entirely beyond Brutus. Has he not just before been playing himself up to, and as against, Cassius? He has been very noble about not taking bribes and not raising money 'by vile means'; his own method of getting it being to send to Cassius for it.

> By heaven, I had rather coin my heart
> And drop my blood for drachmas, than to wring
> From the hard hands of peasants their vile trash
> By any indirection—

All perfectly sincere, no doubt, and as useless, so far as paying the legions is concerned, as it would be for our own Income Tax commissioners. You cannot conduct campaigns in that way. But you can play Cassius entirely off the stage and be left nobly forgiving him, and afterwards venting your irritation on a poet. There seems to be no reason for the incursion of the poet except that he may be kicked out, not by Cassius of 'the rash humour' but by the

> lamb
> That carries anger as the flint bears fire.

But it is in the last act that Brutus comes to be himself; that, perhaps, Shakespeare, having half-certainly and half-uncertainly, touched him all through with 'one auspicious and one drooping eye', sympathetically and ironically, suddenly made up his mind with what kind of poetry to send him into his last battle. Cassius asks him what he will do if they are defeated. The whole passage should be quoted.

Brutus. Even by the rule of that philosophy
 By which I did blame Cato for the death
 Which he did give himself; I know not how,
 But I do find it cowardly and vile,
 For fear of what might fall, so to prevent
 The time of life: arming myself with patience,
 To stay the providence of some high powers
 That govern us below.
Cassius.   Then, if we lose this battle,
 You are contented to be led in triumph
 Thorough the streets of Rome?
Brutus. No, Cassius, no: think not, thou noble Roman,
 That ever Brutus will go bound to Rome;
 He bears too great a mind: but this same day
 Must end that work the ides of March begun;
 And whether we shall meet again I know not.
 Therefore our everlasting farewell take:
 For ever, and for ever, farewell, Cassius!
 If we do meet again, why, we shall smile;
 If not, why then, this parting was well made.
Cassius. For ever, and for ever, farewell, Brutus!
 If we do meet again, we'll smile indeed;
 If not, 'tis true this parting was well made.
Brutus. Why, then, lead on. O! that a man might know
 The end of this day's business, ere it come;
 But it sufficeth that the day will end,
 And then the end is known. Come, ho! away!

Caesar's ghost had promised to meet him at
Philippi, and did not—as we have the play. But
perhaps in fact he did; here, when Brutus accepts
his own nature. Philosophy or no philosophy, he
will not go bound to Rome; this day ends 'the
work the ides of March begun'; the future may
hold victory or defeat; let us deal with the moment
as we may. In recognizing that uncertainty he

comes as near reaching Caesar's certainty as he can.

There is uncertainty and apprehensiveness in the play, as there is deception and self-deception in *Twelfth Night*. 'The rain it raineth every day.'

O that a man might know
The end of this day's business ere it come.

Shakespeare's poetry might well have sighed that last prayer. For it was now on the point of searching deeper states of being, where victory and defeat were to be contemporaneous rather than alternative. It had looked at the shifting nature of man in *Julius Caesar*, and it had to go farther. Brutus, for all his rational resolution, had acted irrationally. But how did man come to act at all?

The problem was not solved, though it was stated, in *Hamlet*. But it will be convenient to leave *Hamlet* for the moment, and consider first what may have been a later play—*Troilus and Cressida*.

III

Troilus and Cressida has always been a problem. It has the signs of a great play, yet it hardly succeeds in being one; indeed it hardly succeeds in being a play at all. No other of Shakespeare's plays so misses a dramatic, a theatrical, conclusion; it ends indeed with the vague statement, by both armies and individuals, 'Well, we'll all fight again to-morrow.' Its love-concern is left as unconcluded, compared to every other Shakespearian love-affair, as its war, and we know that this was not because Shakespeare minded huddling up his characters in order to end a play. Hortensio and the widow at the beginning of his career, Camillo and Paulina at the end, are examples of this. He might not have been able to deal with Troilus—owing to the tradition—quite as easily, but that he should have desired no rounder ending is inconceivable.

Even the theme of Achilles is left unfinished. The policy of Ulysses, by which Achilles was to be brought from his tent into the field, produces no result: he has only succeeded in making Ajax as proud as Achilles, who himself—in spite of Ulysses' medicinal treatment—does not emerge until the death of Patroclus. So, as Thersites says, 'policy grows into an ill opinion'.

These three themes of the play then are abandoned just as the fight between Ajax and Hector is abandoned. But the abandonment is not only on the side of action, but of intellect also.

Troilus and Cressida differs positively from the other plays in this—that there are here two full-dress debates which are not paralleled elsewhere. There are discussions elsewhere, some shorter, some longer; there are the King and his lords in *Love's Labour's Lost* who talk of what had better be done about their vows to study; and King Henry V's consultation of the Archbishop about his invasion of France, and so on. But none of these have, to anything like the same extent, the serious intellectual argument of the two *Troilus* debates. The first is the discussion between the Greek generals about the unfortunate position of the war. It is interesting because the first 54 lines are an example of Shakespeare's wonderful capacity for saying nothing particular at great length—and saying it superbly. Agamemnon opens by saying:

1. Every earthly design falls short of what was hoped.
2. Checks occur in everything.
3. Every action fails to carry out the original intention.
4. These things are sent to try us.
5. They show us what men are made of.
6. We find out by these difficulties which men are really capable of perseverance.

This takes him 30 lines. Nestor then adds:

1. When things go smoothly everybody is happy.
2. But in dark hours we discover who has pluck and who has not.

This takes him 24 lines.

The second debate takes place between the princes of Troy on the Greek proposal (of which nobody up to then has heard a word) that, if the Trojans will give up Helen, the war shall be concluded, without any indemnities or annexations. There ensues then —a thing unique in Shakespeare—a two-hundred line discussion which passes from Helen to an abstract question: What exactly *is* value?

> *Hect.* Brother, she is not worth what she doth cost
>   The holding.
> *Tro.*   What is aught but as 'tis valued?
> *Hect.* But value dwells not in particular will;
>   It holds his estimate and dignity
>   As well wherein 'tis precious of itself
>   As in the prizer. 'Tis mad idolatry
>   To make the service greater than the god.

Here, if anywhere, here, with really good arguments being exchanged, with a philosophic basis and a particular topical example to illuminate it, here we might expect the Shakespeare of whom we heard so much in our youth—the teacher, the philosopher, the sage—to solve for us one of our profoundest problems. How are we to value things? What principle of relativity ought to govern our actions? Shakespeare sets the two arguments, each with its full emotional vitality, against each other, and then causes the protagonist of one side to throw up his whole case. Hector has throughout been insisting that Helen ought to be given up; at the end of the scene we find, not only that he does not intend to act on his own belief, but that he never has intended to act upon it.

Let Helen go . . .
What merit's in that reason which denies
The yielding of her up?

If Helen then be wife to Sparta's king,
As it is known she is, these moral laws
Of nature and of nations speak aloud
To have her back return'd: thus to persist
In doing wrong extenuates not wrong,
But makes it much more heavy. Hector's opinion
Is thus, in way of truth: yet, ne'ertheless,
My spritely brethren, I propend to you
In resolution to keep Helen still;

I have a roisting challenge sent amongst
The dull and factious nobles of the Greeks
Will strike amazement to their drowsy spirits.
I was advertised their great general slept
Whilst emulation in the army crept:
This, I presume, will wake him.

And we are not meant to blame Hector for this; he is not presented as a blameworthy character. It might be argued that his own desire for personal glory is to be supposed to overcome his intellectual beliefs; but in that case, with a consciousness so developed as is Hector's, so vivid and complex a mind, we might reasonably expect to see something of an interior conflict. He shows no hesitation at all at his inconsistency. But as a result of this inconsistency of course the whole discussion stops—'their unanimity is wonderful'. The intellectual arguments then are abandoned—as intellectual arguments— precisely as the action—as action—is abandoned. The whole play is full of this sense of things being left 'in the air'.

It is an old observation, again, that *Troilus* possesses an unusually Latinized vocabulary, sometimes used with an awkwardness which is unlike the normal Shakespeare and at times becomes almost funny. For the most striking examples—

                         Checks and disasters
Grow in the veins of actions highest rear'd,
As knots, by the conflux of meeting sap,
Infect the sound pine and divert his grain
Tortive and errant from his course of growth.

                      Why then, you princes,
Do you with cheeks abash'd behold our works,
And call them shames? which are indeed nought else
But the protractive trials of great Jove
To find persistive constancy in men.

                    'Tis mad idolatry
To make the service greater than the god;

And the will dotes that is inclinable
To what infectiously itself affects,
Without some image of the affected merit.

But I attest the gods, your full consent
Gave wings to my propension and cut off
All fears attending on so dire a project:
For what, alas, can these my single arms?
What propugnation is in one man's valour, . . .

Sith yet there is a credence in my heart,
An esperance so obstinately strong,
That doth invert the attest of eyes and ears,
As if those organs had deceptious functions,
Created only to calumniate.

The voices of these characters labour with an
unaccustomed trouble; their learned minds choose
words with difficulty, instead of their high passion
choosing their words for them. They have a speci-
ously intellectual vocabulary, they toil at defining
themselves in terms of the mind. Their subtleties
are subtleties of argument; they lack the consummation of essential being.

Or almost lack it. For this play, full of abandoned
action and arguments, yet contains one of the very
greatest achieving lines in all Shakespeare, and one
of the most splendid and complex speeches. It
contains one of those moments where the poetry of
human experience is as sublimely itself as ever
before or after. Speech and line both occur in v. ii,
after Troilus has become aware of Cressida's muta-
bility. He is changed; and that change is not only
in him, it is paralleled and expressed by a change in
Shakespeare's own manner. Troilus, like Words-

worth, undergoes an entire subversion of his whole experience—he is given up to 'a conflict of sensations without name'.

To that conflict Shakespeare devoted a speech; but he expressed it also in a line. And that line is no longer an intellectual statement, however thrilling, or a beautiful reverie, however moving—it is a synthesis of experience, an achievement of a style, the style for which *Troilus and Cressida* had been looking.

The crisis which Troilus endured is one common to all men; it is in a sense the only interior crisis worth talking about. It is that in which every nerve of the body, every consciousness of the mind, shrieks that something cannot be. Only it is.

Cressida *cannot* be playing with Diomed. But she is. The Queen *cannot* have married Claudius. But she has. Desdemona *cannot* love Cassio. But she does. Daughters *cannot* hate their father and benefactor. But they do. The British Government *cannot* have declared war on the Revolution. But it has. The whole being of the victim denies the fact; the fact outrages his whole being. This is indeed change, and it was this change with which Shakespeare's genius was concerned.

> This she? no, this is Diomed's Cressida.
> If beauty have a soul, this is not she;
> If souls guide vows, if vows be sanctimony,
> If sanctimony be the gods' delight,
> If there be rule in unity itself,
> This is not she. O madness of discourse,
> That cause sets up with and against itself;
> Bi-fold authority! where reason can revolt
> Without perdition, and loss assume all reason

Without revolt: this is, and is not, Cressid.
Within my soul there doth conduce a fight
Of this strange nature, that a thing inseparate
Divides more wider than the sky and earth;
And yet the spacious breadth of this division
Admits no orifice for a point as subtle
As Ariachne's broken woof to enter.
Instance, O instance! strong as Pluto's gates;
Cressid is mine, tied with the bonds of heaven:
Instance, O instance! strong as heaven itself;
The bonds of heaven are slipp'd, dissolv'd and loos'd;
And with another knot, five-finger-tied,
The fractions of her faith, orts of her love,
The fragments, scraps, the bits, and greasy reliques
Of her o'er-eaten faith, are bound to Diomed.

Troilus sways between two worlds. His reason,
without ceasing to be reason, tells him that this
appearance of Cressida is not true; yet his loss is
reasonable and cannot protest because this is the
nature of things. Entire union and absolute division
are experienced at once: heaven and the bonds of
heaven are at odds. All this is in his speech, but it
is also in one line. There is a world where our
mothers are unsoiled and Cressida is his; there is a
world where our mothers are soiled and Cressida is
given to Diomed. What connexion have those two
worlds?

Nothing at all, unless that this were she.

This is the 'inseparate thing' at a distance from which
the earlier debates took place. Agamemnon and
Nestor had made orations about the disappointments
of life, the failure of 'the ample proposition that hope
makes', and the need of courage and patience.

Ulysses had answered by pointing out that degree and order were being lost, and had described what happens when degree is lost. It was all very wise, very noble, talk. But in Troilus the thing has happened: the plagues, portents, and mutinies have begun to 'divert and crack, rend and deracinate' his being. Order is wholly lost—

> Take but degree away, untune that string,
> And, hark! what discord follows.

> If there be rule in unity itself,
> This is not she. O madness of discourse,
> That cause sets up with and against itself.

The Grecian princes were in dismay and grief— 'what grief hath set the jaundice on your cheeks?' But Troilus, had Hector asked him a similar question, might have answered with Wordsworth

> Grief call it not—['tis] anything but that,
> A conflict of sensations without name.

The conflict is recognized 'with glory not its own' in Troilus' single line.

It might be too much to say that the line is the first place in which that special kind of greatness occurs in Shakespeare; but it is, I think, true to say that never before in his work had such complexity of experience been fashioned into such a full and final line. It is his power entering into a new freedom.

But this freedom is of another kind from the general behaviour of his poetry in *Troilus*. The importance of *Troilus* is that we have Shakespeare's genius, as it were, compelling itself to look for a way of doing things, trying out one way and finding

another. It has been said that he was, in parts of
Troilus, trying to write as Chapman sometimes wrote.
But *why* was he trying for this, if indeed he was?
Because he was trying to press deeper and deeper
into the complexities of experience, and because at
first he tried to do it by a philosophical vocabulary,
by intellectual summary, by argument. He came
near to making 'long orations'; he passed—at a
distance, but he passed—the place where

> opinions every day
> Grow into consequence, till round my mind
> They clung, as if they were its life, nay more,
> The very being of the immortal soul.

The dispute of value is a real and intense dispute,
yet it is abruptly abandoned—not so much by Hector
as by Shakespeare making use of Hector. It is not
there that he must dwell, in the councils of the
philosophers. This is not to be his poetry; a greater
thing awaits him, a thing he has not yet fully attempted
—change in the soul of man. His genius itself
changed; it began to create lines so profound and
intense that they cannot be analysed.

> Nothing at all, unless that this were she—

that he analysed himself. But that was the fore-
runner of other lines, unanalysable—

> She should have died hereafter.

> It is the cause, it is the cause, my soul.

On those lines there is perhaps no better comment
than his own: they admit

> no orifice for a point as subtle
> As Ariachne's broken woof to enter.

If we take another 'problem' play we find a different but related effort.

Measure for Measure, as a play, is not a collapse as *Troilus* was, but neither is it a completeness as *Othello* was to be. It has a beginning, a middle, and an end: only they all belong to different ways of writing *Measure for Measure*. We can recognize in the middle the play of which we heard the beginning; and in the end both that and the play of which we heard the middle. The end is perhaps the least effective—it has less poetry in it than the other parts, but as it is the only end we have we must do our best with it. Isabella is a little badly treated by losing her proper place, but then Angelo loses an entire three-fifths of his play, so she did in fact have her revenge on him. So did Claudio, who, in the middle, occupies Angelo's place, and the topmost peak of poetry in the play.

Yet if one could give up that death-speech for anything, and still more the whole scene of confronting persons and values in which it occurs, it would be for a greater knowledge of Angelo. It is the cessation of all concern with him that makes the play so unsatisfactory. Why—with what poetry did he determine to have Claudio executed? How —in what poetry did he find himself when Mariana left him? It is true he has one speech (IV. iv) summing up both, but we could have done with much more. It was not to be; Shakespeare had moved away from the contrast between the untempted Isabella and the tempted Angelo to the contrast between the still-untempted Isabella and the tempted Claudio. It is this failure of temptation even to tempt her that

makes the concluding threat of marriage from the
Duke so unsatisfactory. What! she whose invio-
lable will desired strict rules in the convent and
accepted the strict laws of Verona, and denied
Angelo's fair promises and Claudio's anguish, she
to fall to a couple of lines from the Duke? 'It cannot
be; it is impossible.' Her entreaty for Angelo's
life shows no lessening of her own imperious self-
possession. Shakespeare might have persuaded us
of a change in her no doubt; the fact remains that
he did not. After the Claudio scene the poetry falls
away into ordinary business, and indeed is often
exchanged for prose. The mere operations of the
play conclude crises originally proposed in poetry.
It is for this reason that Mariana—attractive enough
in herself—is, for the play, unconvincing. No one,
I suppose, is ever quite certain that Angelo treated
her as badly as she and the Duke make out. For the
intense conflict between Angelo's real austerity and
real lust, the precise fact that it does need nothing
less than 'a thing enskied and sainted' to cause his
fall, removes him into a world where beliefs concerning him must be of that same poetic nature.
They must conform to his poetic greatness, and this
the statements concerning him hardly do.

I am a little inclined therefore to suggest that in
Measure for Measure Shakespeare again half-tried
a method which he abandoned. The three great
scenes are not, certainly, arguments in the sense of
the debates in *Troilus*. But they are certainly combats
of values in a manner in which there is nothing in
the following tragedies. The very fact that Isabella
is *not* tempted leaves those combats undecided. She

and Angelo part with their conflict unresolved, and it is more than a personal struggle—it is ethical. We do not merely think 'Will she give way?' We think 'Ought she to give way?' There was certainly no need for Shakespeare to decide; the important thing is that he never so clearly raised such a question again. One may think about Othello, Lear, Macbeth, 'O he's going to—do so and so'; even 'Will he—?' But never 'He ought not to kill his wife', or what not.

Measure for Measure, then, remains poetically, like *Troilus*, an abandoned play. There may be every kind of noble lesson in it, but they have not been discovered by poetry. After it we are no more allowed to say 'What principle should govern man?'; we are to be permitted only to find out how much man can endure and still live. Othello *is* tempted and falls; and we follow him to the end.

As for *All's Well*, it seems to matter less than any. It is more of a play than *Troilus*, for it has an ending. But Shakespeare's genius does not seem to be engaged; Diana's gaiety at the end is a tiresome brightness, and even Helena depends for her praise rather on what other people say than on what she shows us. The Countess is a little too quick to contemplate her son's execution. In short, every-thing—poetry and characters and plot (even this!)—is a little below the Shakespearian par. But there is one great phrase in it, spoken by Parolles after his open disgrace—

> Simply the thing I am
> Shall make me live.

That phrase looks forward to the future: it is the key to Shakespeare's latest poetry.

IV

I return to *Hamlet*. There has been argument whether Hamlet does actually delay to kill Claudius, and if so why. The ghost of Kyd and the ghost of Coleridge have been invoked to explain it. In fact, the only explanations of the delay (if it takes place) which I do not remember to have seen given are two: (1) that the Ghost of Hamlet's father knew his son's nature perfectly well, and intended Claudius to be, not directly killed but, worried out of his mind by having Hamlet's gloomy and threatening figure continually about him. A reproduction of the Ghost's own purgatory round Claudius would be, one would think, a much more satisfying revenge than mere straightforward death; and in support of this view we have Hamlet's dim realization of it in the prayer-scene. The Ghost, after all, must have known how Hamlet would be likely to behave, and it is possible that we have missed the point of the whole play by our failure to attribute sufficient intelligence to that paternal and intimate spectre.

If we abandon this explanation as too (what people call) flippant, there is a more serious possibility, and that is (2) that Shakespeare was not then capable of making Hamlet act, that the development of his genius had reached precisely the point where it was intensely aware of man's distracted mind, of its own divided mind, and was not able to solve the problem. In short, that it is Shakespeare, and not Hamlet, who is seeking the springs of action, and he rather than the prince who therefore here delays.

He made this delay interesting and exciting. It

was part of his greatness that he could, when he chose, make anything interesting and exciting. Whatever state his poetic mind was in, that was the state which he could present to us by thrilling words in the mouths of persuasive characters. But the fact that *Hamlet* is wonderful, and that Hamlet is attractive and repellent at once, does not alter the other fact that most poets are at most times trying to get at something a little beyond their reach, at 'something evermore about to be'. This, in a sense, was Shakespeare's state up to *Troilus*—up even to *Coriolanus*; he is in a continual condition of progress. 'The hiding-places of man's power' are not yet entirely open to him.

Whether—in the circumstances of the play— Hamlet does actually delay may admit of argument. But his continual self-accusations at least persuade most readers and spectators that he does. We are, of course, in a difficulty here; the play has been and is continually presented from Hamlet's point of view. If, for once, it could be shown us from the King's, it might make a difference. If, in that second scene, the dark and ominous figure poised beside the throne; if that first line breaking out in a suppressed savage hatred, making its dreadful half-jeer—'a little more than kin and less than kind'; if the continual danger of the enmity which a pretended dementia (Claudius sees through it) is meant to disguise; if that suppressed savagery and pretended dementia creating almost a real madness; if the bitter stabbing at Ophelia, his mother, and himself—if these things were stressed in their dreadfulness, we might be aware of more danger and less delay. This Hamlet

would be quite as much Shakespeare's, if less
traditionally theatrical. But I think such a produc-
tion has not yet been given us, and we are therefore
still under the effect of Hamlet's own statements
about himself. And Hamlet's view is that he *is*
continually delaying, unpacking his heart with
words.

His own view, his own kind of consciousness,
does not change at least until the last act. He is
throughout in very much the state that Troilus was
to find himself in after he had seen Cressida with
Diomed: the world is executing an appalling outrage
on his whole being. But he neither analyses his
state of mind with such intense exactitude as Troilus
was to do, nor can he discover within himself the
initiative to action. He knows he has it, he sees it,
he talks to himself about it. But seeing it is not the
same thing as getting it to work. He can act as well
as Troilus and in the same way when circumstances
force him—Polonius, the death-warrant, the pirates,
Laertes, the death-scene; just as Troilus makes use
of the Trojan war to relieve his private feelings. But
action from within, action of his own will, is beyond
him. Yes, but Hamlet is, after all, a figure in a play.
To say that he cannot discover within himself the
initiative of action is to say that Shakespeare could
not or would not discover it for him. Is it too much
to say that Shakespeare would not because he could
not? that he made *Hamlet* because he himself was
trying to reach by his genius a poetic comprehension
of the place where men act? I should be perfectly
prepared even to accept the view that when Shakespeare began *Hamlet* he might have intended to make

him kill the King much more adequately, that it was
to be practical and not psychological difficulties
which got in his way. We know—on the testimony
of every popular novelist—that the characters of a
book insist on acting 'on their own'; they will have
their own way despite the author. This must make
the writing of books very difficult, and the ending of
novels almost impossible, since one would think no
character would be willing to commit the happy
dispatch. There is, nevertheless, a certain truth in
this cheap chatter, and the truth is that a work may,
in the working, become a very different thing from
the original intention. It is certainly not beyond
possibility that Shakespeare, whose habit of arrang-
ing his plays seems often to have been casual enough,
should have written *Hamlet* with a continual hope of
'something coming off'—'effort and expectation and
desire', to put it Wordsworthianly: that Hamlet's
character formed itself as his creator found himself
continually disappointed in the effort to find the
'right convincing word'. It sounds an idiotic suggestion, but is it quite impossible that the 'To be or not
to be' speech might arise from just this uncertainty?
Of course it is Hamlet's and refers to Hamlet. But
it is Shakespeare's; might it not unconsciously refer
to Shakespeare? 'To be or not to be'—do we kill
the King or don't we? It has been suggested that the
speech in Hamlet's mouth does refer not to suicide
but to killing the King. It is at any rate just possible
that Shakespeare began the speech in this sense, and
as he worked at it found it more and more impossible
to find out the very words in which Hamlet should
reach determination, more and more necessary to

substitute for a discovery of action a discovery of inaction. It is just possible that this speech is the turning-point of the play.[1]

There had been an uncertain touch in shaping Brutus's own personal certainty; there was now a certain touch in shaping Hamlet's uncertainty. The whole combination of style and subject had slightly shifted. And what this shifting unity demanded, what the poetry that was at once its cause and its result had to find first, was a more intense knowledge of the outraged heart of man, was (in fact) Troilus.

But it may be that Shakespeare deliberately determined to present the Coleridgian Hamlet. But still he must *then* have determined—his genius for poetry must have determined—that for a reason. I submit that the reason brings us back to the same place: he chose to work at a man who did not act (or said he didn't) rather than at a man who did. I submit that he possibly chose that subject because he felt safer with it, more competent to discover it. And (lastly) I submit that this means that his genius preferred to deal with a man looking for initiative rather than possessing initiative because it had not yet the 'liberty and power' to discover killing in poetry.

There is a perfectly definite progression in the presentation of the spiritual act of killing in the plays. In the old happy days when the villain came on at the beginning, and in a burst of magnificent stuff announced that he was 'determined to prove a

---

[1] Though the scene where Claudius is praying is almost exactly Shakespeare saying 'I can't think what words the fellow would do it with. So he can't do it.'

villain', the thing was easy. Richard III, having need
of a murderer, calls to the nearest page and asks if he
knows any one whom gold 'will tempt unto a close
exploit of death'. The page fortunately does, immediately calls him in, and the whole matter is settled
with the utmost celerity and convenience. By *King
John* matters had altered a little, and Shakespeare
had got as far as to subdue the proposal to the two
phrases dropped in Hubert's ear, 'Death' . . . 'a
grave'. The assassination of Caesar is partly taken
out of the realm of individual motives and made a
high matter of state. Even Cassius is moved by
public as well as private feelings, and Brutus,
of course, acts on the noblest possible principles
throughout, with his usual complete sympathy with,
and entire disregard of, other people. But, after
Hamlet, killing is a very different matter. It is
forced on Othello as a result of his own completely
changed consciousness; it is raised in Macbeth
to become an act of the soul. The mysterious
'Third Murderer' who appears from nowhere,
with no preparation, whose utterances only make
the killing of Banquo more certain and easy, is
the climax of murder in Shakespeare: he is murder
itself. He has been taken for Macbeth or merely
another ruffian, but the poetic strength of *Macbeth*
makes him more than that. He seems to be kindred to the Witches and more than the Witches,
to come from another world merely to make damnation sure.

Macbeth himself is rather like Hamlet, a private
individual to whom the possibility of killing is
presented. As a poetic problem the question of right

or wrong does not enter; that the Ghost is 'good' and the Witches 'evil' makes no difference to the difficulty of showing forth the setting in motion of the human will. It is at least partly achieved in the later play by the presentation of it as an act already done—'All hail, Macbeth! that shalt be king hereafter.' But nobody—not Horatio, not the Ghost, not Shakespeare—helps Hamlet in that way: he is left to find his own impulse of action.

Action, after all, is a very difficult thing. The normal acts of our lives are either habitual or compulsory. Either we act as we are used to act or circumstances compel us to some unaccustomed act. The extreme of our choice is to do or to refrain, but the deed is usually a mere variation on our ordinary deeds. After our first youth hardly anything is strange. Take forgery, take arson—the mere acts of writing, of lighting a fire are habitual; it is our knowledge of the result and of civil law that makes the variation. They injure others to our gain; it is an idea to which we are perfectly accustomed and perfectly agreeable. But the finality of killing, the strangeness of the act of killing, impose on us the need for a deeper impulse, an impulse which normally demands intensely vivid circumstances before it can be set in motion, and an intense profit to ourselves from the deed. Of the forgery of the death-warrant for Rosencrantz and Guildenstern we might all be capable. But the necessity laid on Hamlet is even heavier; it is to find out a way to act where his own profit is not concerned—it is literally to act disinterestedly, from free will.

Such a discovery—the presentation of such a

discovery, of such a method of action, perhaps it is
not in the power of man to make. But that the
genius of Shakespeare was searching, if not as
deeply as that (which may be only within the knowledge of sanctity), at least all but as deeply, appears
certain. It was trying to find out—and in poetry to
find out is to express, because expression is its only
way of finding out—the springs of human action,
which are the springs of change. Hamlet, more
than most of Shakespeare's characters up to then, is
shown us as being aware of a changed world; but we
are not shown the change in his own awareness. It
has happened before the play begins and it is not
recalled. Ophelia remembers some other Hamlet,
but perhaps Ophelia is not the most trustworthy
witness. In any case, the event of the actual change is
not presented to us; for that we have to wait for *Troilus*.

It is arguable that a certain acquiescence is to be
felt in the last act; it is on the last act that a great
deal of our 'sympathetic' Hamlet depends. But he
has rather entered the shadow of death than emerged
from the shadow of life. His last private utterance
—the last words to Horatio, except for the great
'Absent thee from felicity'—is a curious one for
Hamlet: 'The readiness is all.' But that readiness
is for what he shall endure, not for what he shall
do. It makes more shapely the end of Brutus; it
is a preparation for the harvest of Lear. It is the
maturing fruit:

> O! that a man might know
> The end of this day's business ere it come;
> But it sufficeth that the day will end,
> And then the end is known. Come, ho! away!

... If it be now, 'tis not to come; if it be not to come, it will be now; if it be not now, yet it will come: the readiness is all. . . . Let be.

> Men must endure
> Their going hence, even as their coming hither:
> Ripeness is all. Come on.

What has to end, of course, is the play. It is to the play's conclusion that Shakespeare is addressing himself; it is that which forces from him an utterance consonant with the nature of whatever character speaks, but consonant also with his genius at that time. I cannot feel that it is entirely by accident that that genius in *Julius Caesar*[1] ended with a desire for, and an expectation of, a certitude dimly seen in the Ghost of Caesar; that directly afterwards in *Hamlet*—before the tragedies—it ended with readiness; and after *Troilus* and *Othello* ended *Lear* with ripeness. Indeed it had reached ripeness then.

Nevertheless, in *Hamlet* the poetic genius was beginning again, like a 'fool of nature',

> to shake [its] disposition
> With thoughts beyond the reaches of our souls;

it also had

> something in [its] soul
> O'er which [its] melancholy sits on brood.

The hint of that is in the King's meditation— 'there the action lies In his true nature'. Until it

---

[1] It is a fantasy—and the Ghost of Banquo comes later to spoil it —but I have wondered whether the Ghost of Caesar and the Ghost of Hamlet's father are a visionary presentation of the visionary power (in Wordsworth's phrase) which was then pressing on him, apparitions of the 'something evermore about to be'.

found out the true nature of action, poetry had still
to absent itself from its felicity. In the words of the
play that was soon to follow, it might have said to
itself

Not poppy nor mandragora,
Nor all the drowsy syrups of the world,
Shall ever medicine thee to that sweet sleep
Which thou ow'dst yesterday.

V

After *Hamlet*, *Troilus*; and in *Troilus* the discovery
of change. This, in poetry, means discovery of an
adequate expression of change, and this again, for
developing genius, means the discovery of a changed
style. Shakespeare's genius essayed this and succeeded: it was the point at which he began to proceed
beyond even the greater poets of our literature.
The remaining plays fall into four groups: *Othello*
and *Lear*; *Macbeth* and *Antony*; *Coriolanus* and *Timon*;
Winter's Tale, *Cymbeline*, *The Tempest*, and *Pericles*.
Each of these groups presents another stage in his
poetry's development—until it had reached its conclusion. The perfect satisfaction of genius is that it
shall serve itself and nothing else; what that meant to
Shakespeare is to be discussed.

All those characters over whom he took any trouble
had always been individualized. But they had been
individuals in a crowd. The plays of *Julius Caesar*
and *Twelfth Night* had carried this possibility to its
fullness; each of them has a group of persons, each
distinct, each unique, each therefore in a sense
alone. But the state of mind in which Hamlet
throughout his play and Troilus in one great scene

find themselves introduced a new result: it made them solitary. They are no longer in a crowd; they are divided from the crowd. Claudius, Gertrude, Ophelia, Laertes, and the rest, are a community. Hamlet is in that community, but separate. Troilus, after his crisis, is not shown in any but a momentary relation to his community, and indeed appears but little; his solitude is therefore unstressed. But the group of plays which followed dealt with an increasing solitude.

Change—solitude—action: these three things, inevitably connected, are the concern of Shakespeare's style from *Othello* through *Lear* to *Macbeth*. The alteration in it, because of its deepening concern, might be shown by the difference between an earlier line in *King John* and a later line towards the opening of *Othello*.

Your sword is bright, sir; put it up again.

Keep up your bright swords, for the dew will rust them.

The first is quiet, steady, watchful, conversational; the second is a quiet incantation, issuing from a spirit apparently complete in itself, aware at once of battle and of peace. *Othello* is full of such incantations; its end is achieved by them. But they have separate elements united in them—the dew contrasts with the swords as the brightness with the rust, and the balance is the balance of which Othello is happily aware in his own nature. His nature is in one respect not unlike Angelo's in *Measure for Measure*, for he too supposes himself to be above the heats of the blood; and so he is, till they are outraged. The young affects, he says, are in him defunct. But a balance which presumes so much is over-rash, as Angelo's remoteness was.

Indeed in the end he is outgone by Iago, whose last two lines reveal the interior strength which Othello thought he had, and had not.

> Demand me nothing; what you know, you know:
> From this time forth I never will speak word.

This is the central silence which permits Iago to be previously so talkative. Few of Shakespeare's characters have so many almost chatty soliloquies. But then Iago is the opposite of Hamlet; he is action incarnate, only he cannot find his own reason for it. Othello has wronged him in the promotion of Cassio; Othello has played him false with Emilia; so has Cassio; he loves Desdemona also—*embarras de richesse*. Actually, if reason for his action is needed, it is probably described in three lines in Wordsworth's *Borderers* (III. 1432–4)—

> Power is life to him
> And breath and being; where he cannot govern
> He will destroy.

Iago has sought to govern Othello (in the matter of his promotion) and failed; he will therefore destroy him—this is his secret determination, and the intellect (as usual) hurries up to provide reasons. He does it by effecting a change in Othello's consciousness of Desdemona. Like Troilus, like Hamlet, Othello is flung into the state where something that cannot be true is true. He swallows Iago's accusations with ridiculous ease, it is true; though Shakespeare makes it convincing (i) by the swift and

orderly succession of his emotions.[1] The progress
from credulity to rejection which (realistically) would
take months here takes minutes. But the progress
is complete; all the stages are here. (ii) By the
terrific outburst of poetry in the mandragora lines
which convince us by merely overwhelming. 'Not
poppy . . . shall ever medicine thee'—it certainly
cannot after that; unmedicined, uncured, unsleeping,
Othello stands before us. (iii) By concentrating
attention on the entire change in him. 'He is much
changed', says Iago, and it is this change which
the divine style of Shakespeare has found. The
mandragora lines are followed, almost immediately,
by Othello's own terrible farewell to his past. He
repeats Troilus's cry:

> I think my wife be honest and think she is not:
> I think that thou art just and think thou art not.

He has lived in one world, and now he begins to
live in another; this is change. The agony of the
existence of both worlds at once is the birth-place of
change. Three great speeches discover the strength
and nature of this state—two directly, one indirectly. The moving force of it is in the speech
concerning the 'icy current and compulsive course'
which sweeps into one of those titular lines that
parallel interior movement with space and distance.
The puerile evidence of the handkerchief is raised
to the level of the crisis by the invention which makes
of it a symbol of time and prophecy and sacred
death.[2]

[1] He had tried the same thing in the first scene of *Richard III*
years before—but then for fun.

[2] The handkerchief speech, it must be admitted, is an extreme

The third cry is when he sees the centre of his being—Desdemona in her new relation to him—'a cistern for foul toads To knot and gender in'. The old world is now a wistfulness, a pity, a tragic sweetness. It is there whenever it is recalled, as old worlds are, merely that Othello may exclaim with the rest of us (as he does in almost those words) 'O if it had been anything—anything at all—but precisely this!'

In the last scene the natural egotism of Othello has achieved in this new world the balance it thought it had achieved in the old. He has left off crying out 'minion' and 'strumpet'; he has even left off saying how hard it is on him, and how he could bear anything except—except what he is asked to bear. He supposes himself to be as free from his own 'affects' as he had earlier supposed himself to be. Then his ostensible desire was to be 'free and bounteous to her mind' (and the play is a comment on how far he really wished this. For if her mind *had* turned to Cassio—); now it is Justice which 'strikes where it doth love'. He speaks exquisite tenderness; but Desdemona sees that 'some bloody passion shakes

---

tour de force. For if it were all that Othello now says it is, would he not, actually, have told Desdemona previously? And if it were not, the sudden invention would, one would think, foil itself. It is one of those instances where Shakespeare's poetry was used to get over his dramatic casualness. The web, the sibyl, the hallowed worms, the mummy are there because the handkerchief must be important, because Othello must feel it as important. And he does; he believes it then; it is true whether actually so or whether (as seems more likely) his own passion creates the belief it expresses. It puts terror and poignancy into his reiterated 'The handkerchief!' But it is—even for Shakespeare—a near thing.

his very frame'; and it is in a burst of outraged selfhood that he kills her.

But let us take the first three lines of this scene—

> It is the cause, it is the cause, my soul;
> Let me not name it to you, you chaste stars!
> It is the cause—

What is the cause? The lines are as perfect as any in Shakespeare, and as effectual. But what is the 'it'? Desdemona's beauty? Desdemona's unfaithfulness? Perhaps, if the 'it' means something of that kind. But the lines are a supreme example of Shakespeare's poetry, and therefore they refer to Shakespeare's poetry. A poet's style is produced by his style, of which the *facts* of his plot may or may not at any moment be an important part. Supremacy rises from supremacy. 'It is the cause'—of what? Of the action that is immediately to ensue. Action had been sought for by Hamlet and not found.

> I do not know
> Why yet I live to say 'This thing's to do;'
> Sith I have cause . . .
> To do't.

He had 'the motive and the cue of passion'. But he could not act on the cue; he could say 'I have cause', but not, like the Pontic sea's icy current and compulsive course, 'It is the cause, it is the cause, my soul'. The lines are spoken in a play and they are the play. They mean, they are, the discovery and the expression—the poetry—of action itself. They are action speaking of itself. They are poetry gathering up into itself all the preceding poetry. To relate them to anything outside themselves is to lessen them; it is necessary to relate everything else to them. Everything else is a preparation or a result of them. Only in the superficial movements of life is action divided from its cause; in the profounder the cause is in the action, until the action has been concluded or has become habitual or has been reversed. Action had been, till now, an unknown mode of being; it is now so far understood that its union with its cause is grasped. And what, in the poetry, is the cause? Why, 'Keep up your bright swords, for the dew will rust them' and 'I loved her that she did pity them' and 'O my fair warrior!' and 'If she be false O then heaven mocks itself'[1] and 'Not poppy nor mandragora' and 'O now for ever Farewell the tranquil mind' and 'The worms were hallowed that did breed the silk' and 'O Iago, the pity of it'. All that poetry is in the 'It'; that poetry is the cause of 'It is the cause'. But why is 'the cause' not to be named to the chaste stars? Because Shakespeare is not talking metaphysics; he is talking Othello. It is not abstract cause and abstract action; it is *this* cause and *this* action—the cistern and the knotted gendering toads. Also because the line shuts up Othello still more dreadfully in his own solitude. It is in that solitude that he utters again: 'It is the cause'. He describes his own words when, a little farther on, he speaks of

the strong conception

That I do groan withal.

It is his action groaning with its cause. But it is

---

[1] Instance, O instance! strong as heaven itself;
    The bonds of heaven are slipp'd, dissolv'd, and loos'd.

not he only who groans; it is Shakespeare. And the true answer to his question:

> Will you, I pray, demand that demi-devil
> Why he hath thus ensnared my soul and body?

would be that the genius of Shakespeare had been determined to discover, by expressing it, a more definite knowledge of the nature of action.

VI

In *Hamlet* the search for action; in *Troilus* the union of concord and discord—two worlds at once; in *Othello* this union driving the hero to action which is one with his realization of that agonizing cause. The fact of that universal contradiction had come to Troilus at the end of that play; to Othello in the third act. But in *Lear* and *Macbeth* it is much nearer the beginning of each play, and each proceeds to find out solitude. *Lear* is the more terrific, but perhaps *Macbeth* is the more awful. For in effect they are parallel and opposite studies—*Lear* of death, *Macbeth* of life.

Othello had had at least a possibility of action; he could, in some sense, reply to the universe that racked him. But the fundamental fact of Lear when he is struck by a similar crisis is that he is not in a position to act. He is man with cause for action yet impotent to act—'I will do such things,—What they are yet I know not.' But Hamlet also had been incapable of action? Yes, but he had not been deprived of all means of action. The difference is between a man who cannot bring himself to act as Othello can and the man who has not the power to act as Othello has. The difference again is between Shakespeare making a poetic thing out of his own uncertainty about the springs of action, and Shakespeare making a poetic thing out of his certainty of what will happen to an imperious nature outraged and helpless. It is a minor point, but worth remarking, that one of the results of Lear's surrender of his kingdom is that he has nothing to do. He cannot be helped by the insistent return of usual daily work. He is in a position where his past habits are no use to him; he is in a void of demanded activity. On the one hand, he has no power to seize his kingdom again, to enforce his will on his daughters, or even to revenge himself on them; on the other hand he is of a temper which forbids any moral or religious acquiescence in the action of the universe. It is a doubtful point—one of those points which are always being urged on one side or another to prove some particular view of Shakespeare—but it might be argued that Albany does represent this point of view. Goneril contemptuously says that 'he'll not feel wrongs Which tie him to an answer': he refuses, that is, to be bullied by the universe into action. It is why Goneril calls him 'a moral fool'. But on his own judgement he takes action—

> I arrest thee
> On capital treason; and, in thy arrest,
> This gilded serpent.

It would almost be possible to imagine Shakespeare's genius proceeding by questions—not that it is likely to have done so but as a way of making its progress clear. (1) When does man act? (2) At his deepest crisis: what is that crisis? (3) This 'thing inseparate' dividing wider than the sky and earth: how does he receive it? (4) He madly avenges himself on the thing which typifies that division: but if he cannot? (5) He will break under it. *Lear* is the breaking, almost the dissolution, of man.

To present that dissolution Shakespeare gathered all figures of madness and unrest. Three forms, with minds distracted, dance in the storm; that one of them only pretends adds, in the subtlety of poetry, to the sense of distraction, for the reader's own mind has to keep this contradiction in memory through all Edgar's wild inventions of madness. There is a multiplication of treacheries and revolts and fidelities, of allied hates and antagonistic loves. Poetry goes to its utmost extreme in denials and invocations of destruction. How small is the time, how few the lines, given to Edmund's relations with Goneril and Regan, yet the whole situation is plain and terrible: even though it is finally defined and magnified in his mighty phrase—'Yet Edmund was beloved.' The play is rich in such synthetic phrases; it is why there is the Fool in it. 'Ripeness is all' is another; that is what Brutus was feeling for.

Things are done and said in a moment, and all the human relations are suddenly altered. The time must spread over months, yet it is somehow all over in little more than two or three nights. Everything is at the worst, yet a voice cries out

The worst is not
So long as we can say 'This is the worst'

and then suddenly there is a different music

We two alone will sing like birds i' the cage . . .

but it does not last, for at the end, more simply than
ever before, the inseparate division of good and evil
returns; now no more of any experience except death
and life—

> No, no, no life!
> Why should a dog, a horse, a rat, have life,
> And thou no breath at all? Thou'lt come no more
> Never, never, never, never, never!
>
> Pray you, undo this button: thank you, sir.
> Do you see this? Look on her, look, her lips,
> Look there, look there!

We have been told that Gloucester's

> flaw'd heart—
> Alack! too weak the conflict to support;
> 'Twixt two extremes of passion, joy and grief,
> Burst smilingly.

Lear dies beholding some similar opposition—not
contest—as it seems to him, between death and life.
But his prophecy was to be true of later plays: 'the
mystery of things' was to go deeper yet, only after
a yet more close bringing together of separate things
in a thing inseparate. Cordelia was dead; three
centuries of critics have talked as if Cleopatra did not
die.

Before Cleopatra, however, there was to be another
solitude. *Macbeth* is one of the most moral of the
plays; it is a tract against murder in a sense in which
Othello can hardly be called a tract against jealousy
or even tyranny, or *Lear* a tract against ingratitude.
From the beginning the sense that something ought
not to be done is as much a part of the play as the

sense that something ought to be done is of *Hamlet*:
it is a kind of opposite of *Hamlet*. Macbeth desires
the intense imagination of sovereignty; what he is
doubtful about is whether the murder will help him
to that. He is quite right; the result in the end is to
remove from him all sense of sovereignty whatever.
Macbeth then is, as the other tragedies are not, a
play of deliberate choice. But it is also something
more.

Ever since *Twelfth Night* (with the exception of
the two comedies, *Measure for Measure* and *All's
Well*) the plays had been dealing with distraction
and ruin in a steadily increasing violence. The minds
of Hamlet and Troilus, of Othello and Lear, are
ravaged until in the case of Lear the play itself is
hardly sufficient to contain the storm. But Macbeth
is not ravaged; he utters no violent farewell to the
past, nor is he either tortured or relieved by insanity.
A different fate falls on him; he is separated from
men and shut up in an infinite tedium.

> Returning were as tedious as go o'er
>
> I have lived long enough
>
> I have almost forgot the taste of fears
>
> . . . I have supp'd full with horrors.
> Direness, familiar to my slaughterous thoughts,
> Cannot once start me.
>
> I 'gin to be aweary of the sun.

These speeches, and the phraseology of the 'To-
morrow' speech—'this petty pace', 'dusty death',
'a walking shadow', 'heard no more'—have all one
burden: unutterable weariness, a conscious somnam-

bulism, a state in which the living mind is aware of
nothing worth while; everything signifies nothing.
What Lady Macbeth becomes corporeally he becomes spiritually. Into this void of shadows only
one sound breaks—the noise of war. Before Duncan
was slain the 'false creation' of a dagger had spectrally
appeared; before Macbeth is killed daggers and
swords are the only actualities that can pierce into
his withdrawn and hollow mind. 'All that is within
him does condemn', says Menteith, 'Itself for being
there.' Menteith, perhaps, had chiefly a moral con-
demnation in mind, but the truth has gone beyond
that. All Macbeth's faculties, except only an instinctive defiance, condemn themselves for being there.
He is still—but now he is only—Bellona's bride-
groom: all other trysts and marriages are done. By
dreadful irony he prophesies the exact truth of
himself when he says, to persuade his hearers of his
distress at the murder of Duncan:

> Had I but died an hour before this chance
> I had liv'd a blessed time; for, from this instant,
> There's nothing serious in mortality,
> All is but toys; renown and grace is dead,
> The wine of life is drawn, and the mere lees
> Is left this vault to brag of.

To this state he has been swept on a 'compulsive
force' moving steadily and with increasing power
throughout the play. Its language, its persons, from
the beginning proclaim that the deed is already done.

> All hail, Macbeth! that shalt be king hereafter.

> Fate and metaphysical aid doth seem
> To have thee crown'd.

Thy letters have transported me beyond
This ignorant present, and I feel now
The future in the instant.

I go, and it is done.

But when it is, the steady movement of fate sweeps
on, invoked by Macbeth—

Come fate into the lists
And champion me to the utterance!

There are still 'terrible dreams'—Banquo's ghost
is all we see of them, and this sends Macbeth again
to the weird sisters. There he becomes a part of
prophecy itself; his safeguards—'none of woman
born'; 'till Birnam wood be come to Dunsinane'—
are in fate, and his safety depends, not on himself,
but on the process of things. Only that process and
he exist, and they are antagonists.

For, setting aside murder as being merely a
decoration of the theme, or at least a secondary
opportunity to make the theme more awful, the
theme itself is action in separation from the universe.
Othello's action is taken distractedly, but Macbeth's
deliberately; for when allowance has been made for
all the pressure of the Witches and Lady Macbeth
there is still left a sense of choice. This is what
keeps Macbeth, even more than his wife, in the
centre of the stage—this and her collapse under
that strain which does but make him, in a sense,
even greater than before. For Macbeth is certainly,
even in that awful somnambulism, yet a greater
mind at the end of the play than at the beginning,
and it is his choice, and the results of his choice, that
make him so. The Witches bring his desired world

vividly into existence; he is aware of two worlds—
one which he does not desire and which is, one which
he desires and which is not.

> My thought, whose murder yet is but fantastical,
> Shakes so my single state of man that function
> Is smothered in surmise, and nothing is
> But what is not.

But it is possible for him to do something about it,
as it was not possible for Troilus or Othello. The
mind of Shakespeare had closed with the idea of a
man acting at odds with the whole nature of things,
and the man's mind and intention must be steady.
It is this steadiness which enables him, from his
own point of view, to see and say that life signifies
nothing: the line is a profound realization, not an
agonized cry. It is this equal movement throughout
the play—'determined things to destiny' holding
their way—which sets *Macbeth* not with *Othello*
and *Lear* but with *Antony*. By now Shakespeare's
poetry had left behind even that supreme crisis of
experience which it had dealt with in the three
preceding tragedies. It was considering man and
that which is other than man. Life signifying nothing
—Having finished *Macbeth* he went on to *Antony*,
in which even death was to signify something. But
he left behind him a presentation of a state of the
extremest conscious solitude possible to man.

Othello had shown solitude and action arising out
of change. But in *Macbeth* the three are one; this is
the inner unity of the play. They are all present
continuously; none is afore or after other, none is
greater or less than another. They can hardly be

divided in thought; if we regard Macbeth from one
point of view we are compelled to see the others at
the same time. He is changing throughout; and
each change develops its action; and each action its
deeper solitude—the separation from Duncan, from
the lords, from Lady Macbeth, from everything.
There is another cause that sets this play with
Antony. However important, however vital, Desdemona and the ladies of *Lear* had been, yet the
plays which contain them had had a single movement
from a single centre. *Macbeth*·has a double centre;
Antony a triple. Shakespeare's genius imagined a
more complex origin for them, it imagined a relationship of individuals rather than an individual in
relationships. The relationship in *Macbeth* is dis-
solved, in *Antony* it becomes more intense; this is
the progression of the poetic mind discovering
fresh powers of knowledge in itself, comprehending
more of 'the wondrous architecture of the world'.

In *Antony*, however, there is no action. 'I speak
as a fool'—but armies and nations, cities and
provinces, queens and emperors, do not make
action. Nor (as we have every reason to know, who
have so many records of the European chancelleries
in 1914) wars and deaths. Nor love-affairs nor
diplomacies. Nor delights nor distresses. But having
said so much, the plain statement may be contra-
dicted; there is action and its name is Caesar, but
at that a modified action, as Caesar himself knows—
'I must perforce', 'our stars unreconciliable'. Caesar
is a great part of Antony and Cleopatra themselves,
as he is of the play. To see him only as antagonistic
to them is to go against his own knowledge. The

play expands from a trinity, not a duality. And
Caesar, for his part, brings into that triune relationship all the earlier power of the 'men of action' but
transmuted. The piety of Henry V has become a
sense of fate; the patriotic glory of Henry has become
a sense of the Roman *imperium*. Unidentifiable multi-
tudes are behind Caesar, whereas behind Antony
are his personal servants. Egypt is taken up into
Cleopatra; but Caesar is taken up into Rome. And
when (as will be suggested) Cleopatra takes up into
herself the Roman spirit of Antony, it helps her
to outsoar the other Rome which is Caesar.

Many adjectives have been used for Shakespeare's
style in this play; no adjective and no array of
adjectives can compass it. It is compact of greatnesses
and nothing but itself can be its commentary. It
is a style which, like Cleopatra, 'makes hungry
Where most it satisfies'. The whole play is itself a
phrase that Ariachne's woof could not enter. But
why *Antony* now? and why *Antony* so? Because
Shakespeare's genius was entering another realm of
expansion. It had found its way to express change
and solitude and action; it was now to discover the
relation of change and solitude and action to something other: which it did in *Macbeth* on the one hand
and *Antony* on the other. It was thus to leave itself
free for its last achievement, which was the approach
to the sheer simplicity of things as they are. But first it
had, so to speak, to get rid of its own preconceived ideas.

So many explanations have been offered of Shakespeare's tragic figures; so much ingenuity has been
spent on attempts to bring them under one law, that
any suggestion must be offered in a deadly fear of

ingenuity. But it does seem as if all the harm that
happens to his chief characters—from Falstaff to
Timon—arises because each of them has some
preconceived idea, some preliminary emotion, about
life, and therefore, largely, about the way in which
other people will behave. Falstaff is certain of the
way in which Prince Henry will behave. He is
armed against the world everywhere but there, and
he is wounded directly through that weakness.
Hamlet has a feeling about the behaviour of widowed
mothers. Troilus has a—rather anxious—preconceived idea on the proper behaviour of a beautiful
young woman who is in love with him. Othello has
it about his wife; Lear about his daughters. Macbeth
has it about the advantages of kingship. Antony
and Cleopatra have it about their own capacity to deal
with themselves and one another and the world.
They all have it; they all lose it; and they all suffer
intensely while losing it.

But a preconceived idea or emotion in the character means a particular intention or approach in the
writer. The things which happen—love, death, or
what not—will happen in a certain way; there will
be a particular response to those experiences on the
part of that complex character. A preconceived idea
makes the character to that extent complex. Romeo's
speech on death and Claudio's speech on death are
dictated by their special characters and circumstances.
So is Cleopatra's. But whereas Romeo's was Shakespeare's genius enjoying itself over death, and
Claudio's was Shakespeare's genius awakening in
us a sense of our own horror at death (especially
death imposed by somebody else's will for somebody

else's moral sense), Cleopatra's is his genius awakening out of an image of death our sense of something quite other than death.

It is sometimes forgotten—or it appears to be forgotten—that Cleopatra dies: she cannot consequently be said to triumph over death. Critics have been excited by that scene (and small blame to them!) to talk as if she triumphed over death. But as a matter of fact she is, when Caesar enters, *dead*; she is a mere corpse. What then has been happening?

This—Shakespeare has been presenting, in the most intense scene of an intense play, a union of intense opposites. The two fatalities of love and death are brought together and inextricably mingled. They are so mingled by a multiplication of lesser opposites. Ideas, images, long words, and short words—all at once are brought into opposition and propinquity. For example—

> the world . . . is not worth leavetaking
> the stroke of death . . . a lover's pinch
>
> Hurts . . . is desired
> knot . . . intrinsicate
> ass . . . unpolicied
> great Caesar . . . ass unpolicied
> lass . . . unparalleled
> Immortal longings . . . Egypt's grape
> fire and air . . . baser life
> warmth in my lips . . . aspic in my lips
> He'll spend that kiss . . . which is my heaven to have
> Give me my robe, put on my crown . . . Yare, yare
> O eastern star . . . my baby at my breast
> O break, O break . . . As sweet as balm
> the luck of Caesar . . . [the gods'] after wrath
> thou . . . and nature

And these opposites serve to convey to us a whole complex of qualities: royalty, immortality, swiftness, mockery, threatening, fidelity, courage, fierceness, lucidity—all these are wonderfully mingled in the first eleven lines. This death is no longer an 'unknown mode of being'; it is known in its fullest extent, as far as anything whatever can be known in poetry.

But this speech is but the climax and close of a play which, in its entirety, is very like that climax. The whole of *Antony* is a union of opposites. Caesar is on one side and the tragic figures on the other, but he is not apart from them; he is indeed the very means by which they, as tragic figures, exist. He and Antony are at one point opposed to Cleopatra; at another he and Cleopatra seem to be opposed to Antony. His passion is opposed to theirs: if we deny him passion—though of another kind—we lessen the play. The manner of Antony's death is opposed to the manner of Cleopatra's. Octavia is opposed to Cleopatra; Lepidus to Caesar and Antony; Pompey to all three; Alexas to Charmian; Ventidius to Antony.

But the greatest opposition is between what Antony and Cleopatra think they are, and what in effect they prove. They are both experienced in politics and love; they both imagine themselves able to deal with politics and love—they have each tried them often enough. And they cannot; their preconceived ideas are destroyed, they are destroyed, by the force which has been awakened. Well, but so was Macbeth, so was Lear: what more could Shakespeare's genius discover?

It had already discovered a way to show man acting according to the cause of his action, and suffering from it; it had discovered tragedy. Such a discovery prolonged itself to the last words of Antony himself—

> a Roman by a Roman
> Valiantly vanquished.

But after his death, and Cleopatra's outbreak over it, her own style changes. She recovers from her swoon as if in it she had lost the accidents and pretences of her state. For a moment there lie together the two unconscious figures—one never moves again, the other moves to a changed rhythm. She has the phrase that no other distracted sufferer had found; not Hamlet, nor Troilus, nor Othello, nor Lear:

> Patience is sottish, and impatience does
> Become a dog that's mad.

Neither patience nor impatience are any good; neither is the resolution of the thing inseparate and divided. But her speech takes on a Roman sound; she has never before spoken to her women as 'My noble girls'; and directly afterwards she uses the word 'Roman' itself—and the word 'noble' again.

> What's brave, what's noble,
> Let's do it after the high Roman fashion.

It may be an accident that Caesar in the very next scene looks forward to her being defeated and a captive by and in Rome—

> her life in Rome
> Would be eternal in our triumph.

But that is not to be the way of union between
Rome and Cleopatra; she is not to live in what is
now but another element in her. She appears again
with a mysterious and profound phrase of poetic
knowledge:

> My desolation does begin to make
> A better life.

Shakespeare's poetry had been up to now concerned with desolation; it began again thereafter to
be concerned with life.

Yet she cannot confine herself to meditation, nor
—actually—does she kill herself because of Antony's
death. The phrase she uses to Proculeius has another
and a vaster meaning than the submission of the
Queen of Egypt to Rome.

> I hourly learn
> A doctrine of obedience.

It is the lesson of the Empress, but also of the
Empress that was

> e'en a woman, and commanded
> By such poor passion as the maid that milks
> And does the meanest chares,

that realization of the strength of the power with
which in the almost ritual colloquy of the first scene
she and Antony had been playing

> I'll set a bourn how far to be belov'd.
> Then must thou needs find out new heaven, new earth.

Destiny took them at their word.

But the play must end, and she must die; and in
fact Shakespeare's poetic sense provided her with

another—a practical—reason for death. Even his
august knowledge refused to determine whether
suicide was, in such circumstances, the right poetic
result of that 'better life' which its awful imagination
saw now in the desolation. Death is forced on her
by circumstances. The fantastic scene with Caesar
follows—led up to by her relapse into a dream[1] of
Antony—in which the old Cleopatra, half-deliber-
ately with Caesar, half-instinctively with Seleucus,
wakes again. The division of the treasure, it is to
be remembered, had been done before; it is not now
accomplished, it is only now revealed. Caesar goes,
and again the word 'noble' breaks out. Then the
crisis of *Troilus* is wholly reversed and resolved.
The domination of that thing inseparate is turned
back, and is dominated by the mind of man, and
poetry which explores the mind of man. The world
which cannot be and which is is here united with the
world which is and which cannot be. Antony is
dead—

> I hear
> Antony call; I see him rouse himself

The poor last of kisses has been given—

> that kiss
> Which is my heaven to have.

Caesar is triumphant—

> ass Unpolicied.

Cleopatra is dying, defeated—

> I am again for Cydnus,
> To meet Mark Antony.

[1] I think this dream-state has hardly been sufficiently stressed;
it is from *that* that she awakes to meet Caesar.

In *Troilus* the two worlds, though too close for
Ariachne's broken woof to divide them, are yet
entirely separate. The distress of Troilus arises
from that intimate separation: his poetry is its
testimony. But Cleopatra's poetry is a thing which
reconciles and unites them. It is not that she feels
herself triumphant; that is not the thing which, for
poetry, matters. The supreme thing in that scene is
the consummation of the poetic mind which here
manages to know those two worlds as one: discovering that knowledge by expressing it. Shakespeare
had known worlds in sequence—values and states of
being; he had known them contemporaneous and
hostile; he now knew them contemporaneous, hostile,
and harmonious. At any time his genius might have
failed; it did not fail. 'Something evermore about
to be' was hardly any longer to be true of its capacity.
Its future was merely what it chose to do; there was
not anything it could choose to be. It had achieved
its own perfection. It might have cried to him in its
joy:

>   Lord of lords!
> O infinite virtue! com'st thou smiling from
> The world's great snare uncaught?

as he might have answered it, looking at the plays:

>   My nightingale,
> We have beat them to their beds.

VII

Coriolanus and *Timon* are, in some respects, alike.
I assume here that they come between *Antony* and
the final comedies, but it is not a matter of much

importance. Their relation to the other plays and
to each other is clear enough, whatever minor
adjustments may have to be made if the correct
dates are ever discovered.

They both to some extent repeat the theme of
Antony in setting up a clash between an individual
and his political world. They both withdraw from
the style of *Antony*, but, of course, *Coriolanus* much
more than *Timon*. They both conclude with the death
of the protagonist, but this death is in neither case
presented with the rapture of Cleopatra's nor even
with the solemn quiet of Antony's. Timon's view
of his own death is that which Macbeth takes of
Duncan's—

> My long sickness
> Of health and living now begins to mend,
> And nothing brings me all things.

> After life's fitful fever he sleeps well.

'Nothing brings me all things' is, no doubt, a
very highly charged poetic phrase. But, so far as
Timon himself is concerned, it is not a phrase
consequent upon 'my long sickness . . . of living'.
Cleopatra—even at her death—never thought of
her long sickness of living; and the 'felicity' from
which Hamlet barred Horatio has in it a more vivid
prophecy of something. Coriolanus is not given a
chance to say what he thinks of dying; he is merely
killed. But neither of the opposing forces which
destroy those heroes—neither Athens nor Rome
and Corioli—are anything like as effective and im-
pressive as the Caesar of *Antony*. He is a worthy
third in his sublime group; but neither Aufidius and

the tribunes nor the Athenian senators are peculiarly
interesting. Shakespeare, for whatever reason, has
taken little trouble over them. On the other hand,
both plays contain an identical theme: in both a
general leads a hostile force against his native city.
Anger has in *Timon* two representatives—Timon
himself and Alcibiades; they divide between them
the rage of Coriolanus. But Coriolanus is melted
and turned aside by his mother: Timon has not a
mother. Volumnia *is* Rome; Athens is given no
such incarnation. May it be partly because Shakespeare could not bring himself to dramatize the
deliberate refusal of the roots and origins of life in
their final showing? Lear curses his daughters, but
—even so—it is the future he would destroy. His
daughters hate and despise their father, but they do
not curse him and their mother is dead. Neither
Lear nor Timon are loosed on the symbolic impersonation of all the past.

But the really curious point is the comparative
poetic dullness of *Coriolanus*. The great change in
him is passed over. He says (IV. i.) on his departure

> While I remain above the ground you shall
> Hear from me still; and never of me aught
> But what is like me formerly.

But the next time he appears is outside Aufidius'
house, and then

> My birthplace hate I, and my love's upon
> This enemy town.

Nor does his speech to Aufidius do more than strike
this note more intensely. The fighting, the civil
dissensions, are effective, but not—for Shakespeare

—thrilling: indeed, one is half-inclined to say, through a great part of the play: 'Shakespeare, thou sleep'st: awake thee.' There is nothing comparable to the apprehension of gold in *Timon* as, not so much gold or even riches but, the medium of man's relation to man, the material symbol of the world's activities, the 'first matter' containing the flow and ebb of created things. But there is Virgilia, and there is the scene outside Rome, and the transcendence of common reunions in 'My gracious silence, hail'. In short, compared with *Antony*, compared with *Timon*, *Coriolanus* is a dull play. It is the turn of Shakespeare's genius after the tragedies as *Troilus* was before, the interspace between apprehension and apprehension; and, like *Troilus*, it contains within it things which are the prophecy of what was to come.

The great things of *Timon* are vehement with conditioned approach. But the great things of *Coriolanus* are mighty with the simplicity of pure existence. Poetry is here purifying itself even from its own dramatic conditions, so far as that is possible. The genius of Shakespeare had been occupied, not merely with the object, but with the way of approaching the object. It had dealt, not only with man's experiences, but with man's varying capacities of knowing those experiences. The capacity was now becoming less and less distinguishable from the experience. Take an example from *Othello* and one from *Coriolanus*—

O my fair warrior!——My gracious silence, hail!

There is a great deal more of Virgilia in the second than of Desdemona in the first: the second *is* Virgilia

but the first is Othello's capacity for knowing
Desdemona. *Coriolanus* and *Timon* were, in the sense
of the quotation from *Timon*, 'nourished' in the same
place, and if we take them together we have another
example of the expanding poetic mind. If we
suppose that *Timon* came first then it seems as if
Shakespeare may have intended to follow *Antony*
by a play in which the dereliction of the central
character was much more final than either Antony's
or Cleopatra's. The 'everlasting mansion'[1] by the
salt flood which twice a day 'the embossed froth
doth cover' is sufficiently far from the profound
imagination of Fate which fills Cleopatra as she makes
her second voyage—'I am again for Cydnus'. But
he found it impossible and abandoned it—in order
that he might give free way to the newly developing
style. He took a similar subject, united Timon and
Alcibiades, and made his first essay towards his
final simplicity.

If, on the other hand, *Coriolanus* came first, then
it looks as if, finding it a comparative failure, Shakespeare made a concentrated effort in *Timon* to get
back to his older style, failed, and abandoned it.
Poets do try sometimes to do what their genius will
not have done; they like what they have been doing
so much that they can't leave it—only they can't
do it. In both plays there is a contradiction, between
Coriolanus and the plebeians, between Timon and
gold. And both contradictions are left unresolved;
the end was not in those plays but in the new
comedies to which he turned. And some such effort

---

[1] Cf. with Romeo's 'everlasting rest'. How romantic the
earlier phrase! how terribly actual the later!

and abandonment remains true even if *Timon* is held to be as early as *Lear*.

In those comedies there are figures which, for all their suffering, do not hate the world. And we have often been told that this shows how Shakespeare himself was reconciled or mellowed or comprehending or what not. It may be so; we do not know. We do not know whether he was ever—for more than the momentary rages which take us all—divided from the world. It is certain that in those comedies he was able, from time to time, to present experience purely in itself. They all—it is a recognized fact—end with pardon, as the *Two Gentlemen* had ended, but with what a difference! That pardon may have been the decision of Shakespeare's own personal mind and spirit: it was certainly, in the plays, the only solution which his style could find for a conclusion. The preconceived ideas of the characters had vanished; and therefore the predetermined methods of approach. Things are but themselves; his genius found that nothing brought him all things. There must then be nothing excluded; and the willingness to exclude nothing must itself exclude only the will to exclude. Such a result means something which, in our ordinary speech, may be called forgiveness; though the thing itself, as we have it in Shakespeare, is too swift, too tender, too lovely for a name which—to most of us—is a rather heavy and solemn determination. The single reproach of Imogen's lifts into a passion of love:

> Why did you throw your wedded lady from you?
> Think that you are upon a rock, and now
> Throw me again.

Miranda is prevented by Prospero with a phrase of dismissal.

> There, sir, stop;
> Let us not burden our remembrances
> With a heaviness that's gone.

In *The Winter's Tale* reconciliation does not allow even an answer of pardon to Leontes' cry 'both your pardons'.

The comedies are too concerned with their subjects to bother about their dramatic arrangement. The seclusion and statue of Hermione in *The Winter's Tale* is, as Alice Meynell unjustly said of the story of the *Ancient Mariner*, 'silly'. *The Tempest* quite frankly falls back on magic. *Cymbeline* adopts the tricks of the earlier plays all over again, as if it amused Shakespeare to recollect his youth—the sleeping-draught of *Romeo*, the separated family of the *Comedy of Errors*, the patriotism of *King John*, the woman disguised as a man of *Two Gentlemen* (and others), the rather caddish young hero of half a dozen, the faithful servant (only young instead of old) of *As You Like It*—culminating in an entirely wild last act of recognitions that even *Much Ado* would hardly have dared. But *Cymbeline* is not a play; it is a person—Imogen. It is Imogen who reduces her own approach to differing experiences always to the simplest words. It is in relation to Imogen that Shakespeare reduces the approach to man's final experience to the simplest words.

'O my fair warrior!'—so, with tenderness and adoration the warrior Othello had attributed his own capacities to Desdemona who (as afterwards appears) is only a little more of a warrior than

Ophelia. She glows in the phrase; she is—for a
moment—transmuted by it. But compare it with
Imogen, when she says to Pisanio, 'This attempt
I'm soldier to.' It is an image, but an image so close
to fact that Ariachne's broken woof could not enter.
Consider the closeness of her approach to the fact
of Posthumus' attitude—

> My dear lord!
> Thou art one o' the false ones.

'No more but so.' She is swift to close with all
facts; she gallops to meet Posthumus, rebuking
Pisanio for sloth; and when she hears of her commanded death she is as quick to meet it.

> The lamb entreats the butcher; where's thy knife?
> Thou art too slow to do thy master's bidding,
> When I desire it too.

Pisanio   O, gracious lady!
> Since I receiv'd command to do this business
> I have not slept one wink.

Imogen   Do't, and to bed then.

The great approach to death in

> Unarm, Eros; the long day's task is done,
> And we must sleep,

is farther off from the immediate knowledge of it
than this. It rejects Pisanio's well-meaning distress
as it rejects fear and delay. All her conversation and
acts are like it; for as Hamlet was the exposition of
Shakespeare's genius seeking for some means of
proceeding, so Imogen is the symbol of his genius
finding a world of sheer experience. In her are
perfectly united the two ways in which, long before,

Shakespeare's genius had divided to express itself. Falstaff and Henry V were not necessary to each other; they were parted and opposed. Caesar and Antony are opposed but not parted. But in Imogen the two images come together. Shakespeare's imagination has synthesized them, and Imogen is the single union. From a similar simplicity comes the Dirge that is sung over her. Shakespeare had 'pursued conclusions infinite' of ways to die. Death had been lamented, feared, hated, desired, scorned, accepted. But never before had it come so near to being nothing but death. The only lingering comment in the *Dirge* is the choice of the word 'Fear'—and that fades from each stanza in turn. The rest is pure fact.

> Thou thy worldly task hast done—

'Unarm, Eros; the long day's task is done.' That line fits its tragedy, but the other fits all things. Poetry there might say of itself, 'Thou hast finished joy or moan.'

If Imogen goes to meet her experience, Miranda need not do that for her experience comes to her. But the art of Shakespeare produced from the solitary girl, when she meets Ferdinand, lines of simplicity equal to the Dirge. Love had been comprehended by as many ways as Death in Shakespeare, from Valentine to Imogen. But Miranda has no faculty for meeting love except love. She *is* love; that is all that can be said.

Miranda   I am a fool
> To weep at what I am glad of. . . .

Ferdinand   Wherefore weep you?

Miranda   At mine unworthiness, that dare not offer
> What I desire to give; and much less take

What I shall die to want. But this is trifling;
And all the more it seeks to hide itself
The bigger bulk it shows. Hence, bashful cunning!
And prompt me, plain and holy innocence!
I am your wife, if you will marry me;
If not, I'll die your maid: to be your fellow
You may deny me; but I'll be your servant
Whether you will or no.

No kind of comment exists there; it is the thing just being. It was this simplicity which Shakespeare carried a step farther in Ariel. Caliban is convincing enough, but Caliban is more native to us than Ariel, whose songs come as near as words can do to suggesting something outside man. The entire lack of any human emotion at all in the 'rich and strange' song of a drowned man; the comparative meaninglessness of the word 'father' in that song; the whole 'sea-change' which his body is undergoing is a hint at a 'sea-change' in poetry itself. A little more, and all our human world would undergo that almost terrifying alchemy, our joys would be pearls, our griefs coral. It has been disputed whether Ariel were masculine or feminine—Ariel! when the very words in relation to him have no meaning. Ariel is only comparable with that other sudden outburst of new awareness, of a different poetic knowledge, when Pericles cries out on hearing 'the music of the spheres'. Shakespeare's poetry imagines that music, as his poetry imagines a note of it, hardly bearable by mortality, in Ariel. It is this which gives a profound suggestiveness to Prospero's speech on the 'insubstantial pageant'. Prospero himself, it may be remarked, ten lines before and ten lines after, is not

in the smallest degree prepared to be such stuff as
dreams are made of.

> I had forgot that foul conspiracy
> Of the beast Caliban, and his confederates
> Against my life.

It seems quite possible that Shakespeare had forgotten it too, and that—having suddenly remembered
it—he created Prospero's speech chiefly to close the
masque and to get Ferdinand and Miranda out of
the way in such a burst of poetry as would leave the
young people (and us) dazed and overwhelmed.
'My old brain is troubled . . . a turn or two I'll
walk . . . Ariel, come! . . . I will plague them all.'
It has succeeded then and since.

> Spirit,
> We must prepare to meet with Caliban.

Yet it has been felt that his speech is of peculiar
significance coming where it does, in the last of the
plays. But that significance is not primarily a
human but a poetic significance. Our awareness of
the baseless fabric of a vision is aroused, of the dissolution of all the actors, and opposed to that is the
music of Ariel. With all kinds and classes of men,
with the great globe itself and all which it inherit,
poetry has done what it can. The elemental simplicities of the last plays, the facts of being uttering
their essential nature, alone remain.

> A terrible childbed hast thou had, my dear.
>
> They have changed eyes.
>
> We knew not
> The doctrine of ill-doing, no, nor dreamed
> That any did.

> You taught me language; and my profit on't
> Is, I know how to curse.

These remain, and Ariel: but no cloud-capp'd towers, or gorgeous palaces, or solemn temples— or anything which belongs to them. So far as all that is concerned poetry will break its staff and drown its book. But that Shakespeare or any other great poet could, finally and deliberately, determine to write no more seems impossible; nor is that habitual allusion necessary. In his last comedies his genius had provided his characters with 'calm seas, auspicious gales', and now it turned to something else: 'To the elements Be free'. It is to the pure elements of this life and of some other that Shakespeare's poetry is now directed; free.

Only he died.

IV

MILTON

I

THROUGHOUT Milton, from the first poem in his
first book to the last choruses of his last, one
subject continually recurs, and that is War. A very
few poems leave this subject for others. *L'Allegro*,
Il Penseroso, a few of the sonnets—these indulge
themselves with quieter things, delighting in circumstances or occupations which for a little are not
disturbed by armed champions. The landscapes
of the early poems are comparable with those in the
Faerie Queene or *A Midsummer Night's Dream*, but
the travellers are of another sort from romantic
wizards or townsmen or fairy kings. A severe and
bright virtue—a young virginity of righteousness—
a beautiful but stern justice—comes shining through
those Miltonic brakes and glades. Of such a kind
are the 'bright-harness'd angels' who sit round the
stable of the Nativity; of such the Lady and her
brothers in *Comus*, and Sabrina. The richness of
the land seems more luxurious around them, just
as the magnificent speech in which Comus urges on
the Lady not merely her folly but her injustice in
refusing the bounties of earth comes with increased
force against her beautiful austerity. The disappear-
ance of these virginal figures is one of the most
marked results of Milton's developing genius; they
recur for the last time when Ithuriel and Zephon
search Paradise for 'some infernal spirit'. After

that we are not shown again 'Virtue in her shape how lovely'. How necessary, how desirable, how final perhaps; but not again 'how lovely'. Christ in *Paradise Regained* hardly makes us feel *that*.

It is then in this double sense that the young genius of Milton set out to enjoy itself—by an intense rendering of sensuous satisfactions and of chastity rejecting them. He—and we—enjoy Comus's palace as much as we enjoy the Lady's refusal. It is delightful to receive the double enlargement of

> No goblin or swart faery of the mine
> Hath hurtful power o'er true virginity.

It is delightful to hear of 'the thousand liveried Angels' that lackey the chaste soul; but it is no less delightful to hear of the evil thing

> that walks by night
> In fog, or fire, by lake, or moorish fen,
> Blue meagre hag, or stubborn unlaid ghost,
> That breaks his magic chains at curfew time.

The poetic union of these two groups of wonders lies in the refusal by the one of the other. This refusal, or its failure, is the subject of practically all Milton's verse.

But with Milton we have neither an account, as with Wordsworth, of the growth of his genius, nor, as with Shakespeare, a mass of poetry covering all his working life. There is in the centre a long suspension, covered, no doubt, to some extent by his prose. But we are not concerned with his prose; only with what his poetry did, and the witness it bore in itself to the place where ' 'twas nourisht'. The two

groups of which that poetry consists are therefore
unconnected. But they are undoubtedly connected
by their theme, and the theme at the end as at the
beginning is war. The crash of the Philistine theatre
on Dagon's feast concludes a battle which 'the helmed
Cherubim and sworded Seraphim' had long before
begun. The only question that can be asked would
seem to be—is it the same battle?

In one sense, of course, it is; it is the battle
between (what Milton thought was) good and (what
Milton thought was) evil. It is even a battle, at the
very end as at the very beginning, between God—
the word throughout this essay means the God of
Milton's poetry and nothing else—and false gods.
Dagon had had a scornful line in the *Nativity Hymn*:
'with that twice-battered god of Palestine', and the
poetry returns—twenty-six years afterwards—to
describe something very much like a third battering.
During those years the war had been carried on in
many places. In the *Nativity Ode* it is in the stable
at Bethlehem, a foreseen spiritual conflict. In
Comus it is between indulgence—especially gluttony
and drunkenness—and a severe temperance; and the
place is in a romantic English landscape. In *Lycidas*
it is between selfishness and duty, and the place is in
the churches and public heights of England. In
the *Sonnets* it is in the Vaudois or the literary world
of London, or it is part of the Civil War (or rather,
the Civil War is a part of it). In *Paradise Lost* it is
enlarged or restored to its original greatness, to
include the whole time and space of the created
universe. In *Paradise Regained* it is localized to a
particular intellectual duel between the protagonist

on either side in a special time and place. In
Samson it is reduced again to its human aspect in
Philistia centuries before Christ.

As a result of this continued concern with an
everlasting struggle, Milton has been accused of
dualism, and no doubt this, in a semi-philosophical
sense, is true enough. It may very well be that
English poetry will never be quite happy until its
thought has retrieved a unity which Milton seriously
harmed. Since Milton philosophical poetry has not
been altogether successful in returning towards that
unity. Pope was a very fine poet; but his pathetic
repetition of 'Whatever is, is right' is silly. Wordsworth was prevented from justly fulfilling what
perhaps he alone could have fulfilled. *The Ring and
the Book*, great poem though it is, fails on the
metaphysical side. *The Dynasts* merely denies both
sides. Somehow we may have to get back to pre-
Miltonic ideas—in fact, to Shakespeare. But that is
only as regards our more or less conscious philosophical business. In Milton's own poetry the division
has its own union; for the war is the reconciling
thing. If the Lady had said to Comus, 'I have my
own views, but I don't say they're right for you';
if God had given Satan a little bit of void to play with,
it might have been becoming in them, but there
would have been no poetry. The war brings them
into touch.

But what is the war about? To answer that question is to follow the curve of Milton's genius, from
its undetermined modes of being to the hiding-places
of its power. But these phrases mean something
different in him from what they did in Wordsworth

or Shakespeare; and the first difference is in the fact
that he was much more deliberately an artist. He
'arranged' much more than those other poets did.
He arranged *Lycidas* as he arranged *Samson*, and
Paradise Lost as much as either. Consider how
Lycidas turns and returns on itself both in sound and
sense; it ascends in spirals. It can even be plotted,
as follows:

Introduction 1–5; lament 6–24; pastoral note
25–49; first questioning 50–63; first parenthesis
64–90; second questioning 91–102; second parenthesis 103–31; pastoral note 132–53; lament 154–
64; conclusion 165–85; epilogue 186–93.

Comus indeed may be said to be full of undetermined modes of being, being full of magical detail.
Comus himself is the child of Bacchus and Circe,
and is what he is by his mere nature, without any
question of choice. He casts spells into the air to
deceive the Lady; against him the Brothers are
protected by the herb Haemony; the Lady cannot
be released except by the use of Comus' wand to
reverse his spells, or by the miraculous intervention
of Sabrina. Even the extreme loveliness of the
speeches on chastity, with their revealed transmutation of all the senses into immortal being, leaves a
mystery in the virtue of which they speak.

The magical detail, the nature of Comus, the
half-esoteric doctrine of virginity—these are the
undiscovered secrets of Comus; undiscovered to us
because undiscovered by Milton's poetry. The
poem acts by magic; it touches us with 'chaste
palms, moist and cold'.

Lycidas, if it does not explore farther, does

definitely point to other places of exploration. It is, in some sense, a prelude to *Paradise Lost*. 'Fresh woods and pastures new'—but that is the language and place of Milton's past occupation. It is in those other lines that the prophecy is heard, in their sound and in their statement.

> For so to interpose a little ease
> Let our frail thoughts dally with false surmise.
> Ay me! Whilst thee the shores, and sounding seas
> Wash far away, where'er thy bones are hurled,
> Whether beyond the stormy Hebrides
> Where thou perhaps under the whelming tide
> Visit'st the bottom of the monstrous world;
> Or whether thou to our moist vows denied
> Sleep'st by the fable of Bellerus old,
> Where the great vision of the guarded Mount
> Looks toward Namancos and Bayona's hold,
> Look homeward, Angel, now.

The Angel of Lycidas might; the Angel of Milton's verse could not. 'The guarded Mount' faces, far off, that other Mount in heaven around which the 'Thrones, Dominations, Princedoms, Virtues, Powers' displayed themselves. And 'the bottom of the monstrous world' has already in it a sense of metaphysical prophecy: 'bottomless perdition' is to be found there,

> Where all life dies, death lives, and nature breeds,
> Perverse, all monstrous, all prodigious things,
> Abominable, inutterable, and worse
> Than fables yet have feigned, or fear conceived,
> Gorgons and Hydras and Chimaeras dire.

Even the God is changing. Jove in *Comus* was no doubt supreme, but he and his servants are only concerned with those mortals who 'aspire'; 'but for such' even the Attendant spirit 'would not soil these pure ambrosial weeds'. They are all away beyond the starry threshold. But 'all-judging Jove' in *Lycidas* is—all-judging. He pronounces on each deed; he is (one feels) in relation to St. Peter and the two-handed engine. He is still solemn, beautiful, credible, but a little aged, a little more concerned with rewards and punishments, a little more driven to make use of mortal weapons: in short, a little nearer the Deity of *Paradise Lost*.

Lycidas is a lament for Edward King. But it is also a calling to remembrance of Milton's young poetry, a lament, a farewell. No wonder it hesitates by Amaryllis and Neaera; the laborious days it foresees are of a different kind to those which virtuously enjoyed themselves contemplating virtue in *Comus*. No wonder it interposes 'a little ease'; *Paradise Lost* would have no room for faint thoughts or false surmise.

Lycidas is a lament, and great authority has declared that it is not a quite sincere lament. What is more certain is that it is a conscious, a self-conscious, lament. Such a self-consciousness had been in Milton's verse from the beginning. The *Nativity* poem inquired of itself whether it had no gift for Christ—many such poems by other poets had similarly inquired and been themselves dispatched in answer. But Milton's was ceremonial, and it was ceremonial because it was self-conscious. One of the advantages of ceremony, rightly used, is that it gives a place to self-consciousness, and a means whereby self-consciousness may be lost in the consciousness of the office filled or the ritual carried out. The art of Milton's poetry is its self-consciousness absorbed in ceremony. *L'Allegro* and *Il Penseroso* also had been conscious—though in their respective ways less ceremonial—the Lady and the Brothers are self-conscious. In one of the sonnets his poetry is already rebuking itself for its unfruitfulness, and pledging itself to that same lot 'Toward which Time leads me, and the will of Heav'n.' A less solemn self-consciousness appears in the Sonnet to the Captain or Colonel or Knight at Arms. The whole of Milton's early poetry—or almost the whole—had this element in it, and this element, being a natural and inevitable part of it, proceeded on into *Paradise Lost*. But there it did more, for there it was not only an element in the poetry, but it became the subject of the poetry. The war in *Paradise Lost* is a real war, but it is also the means to something else, it is the method by which this self-consciousness is fully explored and revealed.

It is sometimes forgotten that Milton did not say he was going to justify the ways of God to man— not like that. He said

> That to the heighth of this great argument
> I may assert Eternal Providence,
> And justify the ways of God to men.

He said it in poetry; that is, his poetry said it; and what poetry says depends on what poetry is being *at that time*, and on nothing else. For what poetry says *is* the poetry. It is not and cannot be concerned with anything but itself. Nor shall we, reading those lines, expect this poetry to fulfil its own desire after any style but its own. We shall not expect intellectual justification—though our intellects must not be offended. Nor moral, though whatever scheme of morality be implied, whether our own or not, must be of a high and enduring sort. We shall, in fact, require only that those three lines shall prelude a sufficiently satisfactory sequence; in short, that the poem shall justify itself. Doing that, it will come as near justifying the ways of God to man as anything can.

This poetry, then, was to assert, to sound, Eternal Providence. But, as nature-poetry is not nature, and love-poetry is not love, so religious poetry is not religion. It may convey religious teaching; it may express our religious emotions; it may make us religious. But in itself, like all poetry, it is the result of a process which Milton, at the beginning of *Paradise Lost*, attributed to the Spirit of God at the creation. The genius of a poet

> [sits] brooding on the vast abyss
> And [makes] it pregnant.

This is what Milton's genius proposed to do; the abyss was to be pregnant with justification.

But though war is the narrative subject of *Paradise Lost*, and justification is the poetic subject, the intellectual subject is Free Will. 'Of man's first disobedience', what moved our parents 'to transgress his will'—this is stated to be the theme. The words 'free will' recur continuously through the poem. But to express what moved our parents to transgress, it is necessary to express how our parents could be moved to transgress—what are the very springs of action. If this is so, then, at the opening of *Paradise Lost*, we are in a similar state of poetic effort to that in which Shakespeare was when his genius was trying to discover, by expressing it, the cause and the manner of the action of men. Only the poetry of Milton knows and asserts what it is about; the poetry of Shakespeare—formally—does not. Nobody knows whether Shakespeare himself knew or not. But his great figures express each a state of being; Milton's figures express their own conscious knowledge of their states of being. They have, in fact, no other subject of conversation; which is perhaps why they do not converse. They do not even argue. They tell one another, but that is not quite the same thing. There are orations, proclamations, prayers, challenges, taunts, inquiries, expositions, defiances, judgements. There is, in fact, everything except conversation. What does God talk about? Himself. What does Satan talk about? Himself. Adam? Himself, as far as possible, but, as he has neither omnipotence nor experience, he is driven back on talking about himself in relation to Omnipotence, until after the Fall. After the Fall he has something more to say about himself, for something more has happened to him, and he says it. And all this talk revolves round two centres—Satan's choice and Adam's choice, the double exercise of free will. Given the narrative-subject of the poem, there could be no other philosophical subject.

By several necessities, then, Milton's poetry comes before us as a self-conscious poetry. It is epic and not dramatic; it is doctrinally epic; it insists, by its arrangement and by the august art of its verse, on its own attention to itself; its chief characters make long and involved speeches about themselves; its chief subject is an understanding of free will which involves an understanding of the nature possessing free will. But the myth of the story involved two chief characters having free will (the subordinate devils may be regarded as typified in Satan, and the good angels do not add much to the exploration; except in one marvellous phrase of Raphael's which will come in later). One of them had all the advantages. He had, when the story opens, experience; he had complexity. And his exercise of will was the primary cause of the exercise of will in the other. Inevitably, therefore, Satan took the chief place.

When Shakespeare was seeking the cause and manner of man's action and had not yet succeeded he made *Hamlet* out of the pother. When Milton was seeking the centre of man's knowledge of himself (in will and action) he made Satan. Of course, Satan is not Milton; Hamlet is not Shakespeare. Milton need no more have approved Satan's character than Shakespeare need have approved Hamlet's. But certainly it is Satan in whom the farthest determination of hitherto 'unknown modes of being' is carried out, and 'the hiding-places of man's power' are so far known.

This determination was carried out in blank verse, and Miltonic blank verse at that. The importance of this fact—sometimes overlooked—is that there is carried into the very form of the poem something which corresponds to the described Omnipotence of God. Everything exists within that dual control. All happens under the Eternal Eye, but

all happens also within the bounds of that great
decasyllabic progress. Satan is a rebel against God;
but he is in some sense a rebel against the blank
verse also. It is true he talks it; that is theologically
accurate. Satan can only rebel in virtue of the
strength that God has given him. 'Immutable,
immortal, infinite', that overwhelming style rolls on.
It is at times almost impossible to leave off reading
it; the verse drags after it the protesting weakness of
the reader's mind.

The first hundred lines of the poem present and
sustain their subject. For *Paradise Lost* opens with
the presentation of the most terrific 'change and
subversion' in English verse; terrific in the fact
described, terrific in the language used.

> Him the Almighty Power
> Hurled headlong flaming from th' ethereal sky
> With hideous ruin and combustion, down
> To bottomless perdition, there to dwell
> In adamantine chains and penal fire,
> Who durst defy th' Omnipotent to arms.

Not only has this united the verse with the idea—
or (to put it more exactly) not only has the poetry
discovered itself in its strength of domination, but
it has also raised the problem which it has to solve.
'Who durst defy th' Omnipotent'—compared to
this Adam's later effort to dodge the Omnipotent is
pathetic. But, sooner or later, it is impossible to
avoid asking Milton *why* the myth should be thus;
isn't it stupid? Who could, who would, defy Omnipotence? Milton cannot, of course, escape by saying,
'Well, that's an old story'; he must make that old
story convincing.

His logical answer is given in the Fifth Book
(ll. 856–63). The rebel angels imagine themselves
'self-begot',

> the birth mature
> Of this our native Heaven, ethereal sons,

and they imagine God to be of the same nature, only
more powerful. Exactly how much more powerful
they may reasonably proceed to try and find out.
But though this is rational, it is by an irrationality
that Satan is shown us. Omnipotence is engaged
upon something to which Satan is with his whole
being antagonistic. Reason bids him submit—God
and Raphael both point this out: even after his fall
from Heaven he considers the possibility. To do
that, however, would be precisely to lose *himself*; he
would be something other than he is. He must act
from what he is, and he expresses this in a minor
contradiction. When he is addressing his followers
he points out that none of them will envy him his
throne; no one will want 'the greatest share of endless
pain'. Reasonable enough, true enough; only it is
precisely this which he himself must demand.
'Better to reign in Hell than serve in Heaven.' This
contradiction is not deliberate deceit; it is the
irrational strength of his nature, which his own inner
force has precisely 'made supreme Above his equals'.
His various speeches on this are united in his
soliloquy on Niphates. There the deliberate acquiescence in a divided consciousness is made, and it is
made because 'he can no other'. Submission itself
would produce no other result than a repetition of
the past revolt. Both he and God know this; there
is between them no smallest possibility of agreement.

It is expressed in the poem by his knowledge that a new world has come into existence in his place—

> behold, instead
> Of us out-cast, exiled, his new delight.

It is a phrase which Troilus, could he have talked Milton, might have used of Diomed. No circumstances could be more different; no essential agony could be more alike. Troilus rushes to arms against Diomed; Othello—more fully expressed—murders Desdemona; Satan makes war on God and man.

> It is the cause, it is the cause, my soul.

It is a state too well known to man. The skies and the abysses, the archangels and chaotic powers, of this poem are not necessary to our recognition of it; nor by them is our capacity for a similar choice awakened. The corner of a suburban road, a metropolitan doorway, are equally adequate surroundings; were those others necessary *Paradise Lost* would be more spectacular and less essential poetry. Milton stresses the moral choice in the contradiction, the choice which so many men have made, the preference for the existence of their own will as the final and absolute thing as against the knowledge (whatever that may be) of some 'great commanded Good'. The only choice which a man can make in such a crisis is between submitting to that good or refusing to submit to it, and if he refuses to submit he does so precisely because so, and so only, he can hold 'divided empire with heaven's king'. Every bold bad baronet in the old stories did the same thing. He cannot get rid of the good, he cannot destroy it.

He can only know, and refuse, and hate it, and be equivalent to it.

So Satan accepts the contradiction within him, with no hope of its resolution and no fear of its agony.

> So farewell, Hope, and with hope, farewell Fear;
> Farewell, Remorse; all good to me is lost;
> Evil, be thou my good; by thee at least
> Divided empire with heaven's king I hold.

The divided empire means double consciousness within him for ever. His own self-consciousness accepts and includes that.

Compared to Troilus, Othello, and Lear, this is a self-conscious state, and involves a moral choice from which those distracted figures are free, for to them, as they are presented, the moral choice is not offered. The question of their duty is not raised: at least, I suppose no one seriously blames either Troilus or Othello (justified and unjustified as they respectively are) for not following some lovelier course of action. Nor Lear. Shakespeare is intent on tracking out the paths by which human nature wanders in 'the dark unbottomed infinite abyss'. Milton reflects also the intense consciousness of himself that takes him there. But Shakespeare's explorations took him to the imagination of a dual and rapturous knowledge, and after that to new life. Milton's went at once farther and less far.

This, at any rate, after the long suspension, was the changed capacity of Milton's verse in its re-issuing. Comus had had no such complexity, nor any such self-consciousness and self-decision. There had been shown in him no possibility of choice, and even the Attendant Spirit was bound to admit that his followers did, as a matter of fact, 'roll with pleasure in a sensual sty'. But this being the common desire of humanity, and Milton's own verse having at least walked with pleasure in a sensuous palace, the two opposite states of being are contemplated as opposite persons. In Satan they are one.

But if this created complexity is one greatness of the poem, there is another in the rapture that proclaims its doom. Satan accepts both evil done and evil suffered, rebellion and pain, not merely the evil of his own will but the evil which that will involves. It is in his choice of both that he holds the divided empire, and is (so long as his vital spirit lasts) something God cannot be; he is as unique as God. But this 'evil' then must be expressed in its fullness. Satan would not be the figure he is if the poetry failed here. The poem would not be the poem it is if its poetry did not discover, as it were, God's consciousness of Satan as well as Satan's consciousness of God. And this can be done even better by the narrative than by the Omnipotent Victor. A self-conscious Omnipotence, a self-conscious and victorious Omnipotence, is a figure which poetry itself can hardly make attractive. And even Milton appears to have been aware that God ought, sometimes, to be attractive.

The narrative therefore gathers itself into intense verse to overthrow the intensity which proclaimed itself within it. To 'Evil, be thou my good' it answers 'be *thou* my evil'.

> Him the almighty Power
> Hurled headlong flaming from th' ethereal sky.

So spake the Son, and into terror changed
His countenance, too severe to be beheld,
And full of wrath bent on his enemies.

Hell heard th' unsufferable noise, Hell saw
Heaven ruining from heaven.[1]

Hell at last
Yawning received them whole, and on them closed,
Hell, their fit habitation, fraught with fire
Unquenchable, the house of woe and pain.

The spirit which inflicts, the spirit which endures, have both accepted the 'thing inseparate'. Between God and Satan, divided 'wider than the sky and earth', yet there is no orifice. This is the conclusion on that subject of *Paradise Lost*.

But in what sense, then, can there be justification in this poetry? The verse has been raised to its height to deny something which the tremendous power of the verse continually expresses. Chaos itself never came nearer discovery than in the description of Satan's awful journey through it. But the poem itself tempts

with wandering feet
The dark unbottomed infinite abyss.

---

[1] It is not in the meaning of the verse except by accident; but it is precisely 'heaven ruining from heaven' which describes the crisis involved. Compare Troilus again—

Instance, O instance! strong as Pluto's gates;
Cressid is mine, tied with the bonds of heaven:
Instance, O instance! strong as heaven itself;
The bonds of heaven are slipp'd, dissolv'd, and loos'd.

and Othello:

If she be false O then heaven mocks itself.

How can it

> like a weather-beaten vessel hold
> Gladly the port, though shrouds and tackle torn?

The answer is that its port is threefold: (1) the other militant solitaries, (2) Eden in Books VII and VIII, (3) *Samson Agonistes*.

Having created Satan, Milton's poetry had to do something else. It had—if there was going to be any more of it—to discover some other way of existing, but (inevitably) some related way. It had also to deal with Adam who was the ostensible subject. By the end of the Fourth Book, Satan had been sufficiently achieved; indeed the episode of the 'back-chat' between him and Gabriel at the close of that book is, in a sense, a luxury. It recapitulates, condenses, and emphasizes all that has gone before —defiance, selfhood, and compulsion by superior power.

> [Satan] fled
> Murmuring, and with him fled the shades of night.

And now what was going to happen?
The end of Book V answers with an exact parallel —the Seraph Abdiel turning his back

> On those proud towers to swift destruction doomed.

Satan chooses evil—Abdiel chooses good; and Milton conscientiously (and quite unsatisfactorily, for the first four books had done their work so well that only Milton's strength of imagination could have invented this episode) allows Abdiel later on to overcome Satan in single conflict. But the trouble is that though this choice and heavenly

defiance is a marvellous piece of work, though the
'Unshaken, unseduced, unterrified' has become one
of our most glorious possessions; though the corresponding line 'All night the dreadless Angel unpur-
sued' has immeasurable distance in it, and is a brief
—and yet infinite—parallel to Satan's own journey
through Chaos—yet the poetry has not discovered
anything different. *Plus ça change, plus c'est la même
chose*—only rather less profound. For the choice is
not as effective as Satan's. Obviously not, since
Abdiel's choice, however difficult at the moment,
will involve nothing like the acceptance of 'infinite
wrath and infinite despair'. Milton therefore cannot
let himself go over it. It and he are circumscribed
by the heavenly host. And even Milton hardly
succeeded in making the heavenly host—or the
hymns of the heavenly host—interesting. If one
could skip in Milton it would be occasionally one of
the choric odes to God. Abdiel, like the Lady in
Comus before him, has to be one of the lesser defiances
that surround, in Milton's work, the figure of Satan.

But there is, if not another solitary, at least the
prophecy of another solitude in the foretold solitude
of Christ. From the beginning this solitude is set
in opposition to Satan's. The silence of Pande-
monium is the counterpart of the silence in heaven.

>   All sat mute,
> Pondering the danger with deep thoughts;
> . . . none among the choice and prime
> Of those Heaven-warring champions could be found
> So hardy as to proffer or accept
> Alone the dreadful voyage, till at last
> Satan

> All the heavenly quire stood mute
> And silence was in heaven: on man's behalf
> Patron or intercessor none appeared,
> Much less that durst upon his own head draw
> The deadly forfeiture . . .
> . . .had not the Son of God.

In spite of this equivalence of virtue it remains true that the choice of Christ is not to the reader of the same imaginative greatness as the choice of Satan. Yet the likeness between Christ and Satan, so expressed, is more than a comparison in mere narration; it is more even than a moral comparison. It is, or it contains within it at certain moments, a psychological comparison. At the end of the Sixth Book, where the Son, riding in 'the chariot of Paternal Deity', casts the rebel angels out of heaven, the description of their overthrow imagines not merely a mythical but an individual defeat. The spirit that rejects the Good is tormented by the Good that it rejects—the shaking of its whole being (all but the 'Throne itself' of that Good)—the infixed plagues —the tempestuous arrows—the glaring eyes—the collapse of all energy, leaving it 'exhausted, spiritless, afflicted, fallen'. Fear and pain and arrows of desire and the strong sense of being a spectacle of mockery and impotent affliction—it is not necessary to turn to legendary battles to recognize those signs. *Paradise Lost* is in its two themes a contrapuntal harmony. The story of the rebels turns back on itself: it opens in hell after their fall, describes Satan's exploration of chaos, and his arrival in Eden, goes back to recount their revolt and expulsion, and then concludes with their local victory and transformation into hissing serpents. But the psychological presentation is continuous; the spirit which in the opening magnificently rejects is itself overwhelmed by the rejected, and after that greater failure boasts of its lesser triumph, before it finds even in that only 'hatefullest disrelish'. The figure of Satan himself, however, is not specifically mentioned in the overthrow; whenever he is defeated it is as a demigod should be; and when he becomes a serpent he is 'still greatest'—

> his power no less he seemed
> Above the rest still to retain; they all
> Him followed.

Milton may have disapproved of Satan but he certainly had an artistic—if no other—tenderness for the 'archangel ruined'.

Attracted by this artistic tenderness the rest of us have rather neglected to attend to the lines which describe—which discover and express—Christ. 'The grand foe' has lured us after him poetically, partly no doubt because our own natures are much more like his complexity than Christ's singleness. But also because he is the most successful example, in *Paradise Lost*, of 'the impersonated thought', which Wordsworth formulated as a maxim. In him the impersonation and the thought are equal. But in God and in Christ the impersonation is much weaker than the thought. They are indeed almost abstractions, and perhaps *Paradise Lost* would be easier to read if we frankly accepted them as abstractions. God would be more comprehensible, even more probable, if we took him to be but a mode of the Good; Christ would be more comprehensible—even as the Sole-

Begotten Son—if we regarded him simply as a mode of the Will accepting the Good. In that way, though he would remain less thrilling than Satan, he would be equally important and exalted, even poetically. We need not deny Satan his extra impersonalization, so long as we allow to Christ his full place as 'an idea or abstraction of his kind'. The poem demands so much; it provides so much. It is for us to recognize that it provides what it demands. Thus the relationship of the Son to the Father becomes credible and beautiful; the great lines which utter that relationship, of the Will perfectly free accepting the Perfect Good, expand within us into something like their power of full communication:

> He said, and on his Son with rays direct
> Shone full, he all his Father full exprest
> Ineffably into his face received,
> And thus the filial Godhead answering spake.
>   O Father, O Supreme of heavenly Thrones,
> First, Highest, Holiest, Best, thou always seek'st
> To glorify thy Son, I always thee,
> As is most just; this I my glory account,
> My exaltation, and my whole delight,
> That thou in me well pleased declar'st thy will
> Fulfilled, which to fulfil is all my bliss.

We have tended to repeat other lines rather than those; we have tended to concentrate on the devil rather than the God. But then in *Paradise Lost* the devil is a lonely figure and the God is not, until the devil succeeds. It seems as if there were in the triumph in Eden something which, while leaving Satan's character as effective as ever, yet opens up the possibility of other defiances. You cannot, it

seems, win a victory without running the risk of a
rebellion; or only if that victory is the secret desire
of the overthrown power—and this perhaps is the
difference between man and Satan. But I think that
is not in Milton, nor perhaps even in Shakespeare.
The journey of Satan from Hell through Chaos to
Earth is paralleled by the departure of Adam and
Eve from Paradise through Eden to their future,
and their future is Christ. Satan's determination is
manifested in action, but the action must have a
result, and the result is still to be explored. Thomas
Ellwood has been blamed often enough for his question, 'What hast thou to say of Paradise Regained?'
But, in so far as the conflict of contradiction in the
consciousness of Satan, of Adam, is not resolved,
but remains as a final accepted choice, Ellwood was
perfectly right. Christ is to solve it; he is aware of
his own future acts; he is aware that he will do so.
But he is not aware of himself in the immediate
knowledge of union as Satan was aware of himself
in the immediate knowledge of contradiction.

In effect, and in Milton, he never was. But in
Paradise Lost he is a place of prophecy, a hiding-
place of man's power.

The second answer is Eden. Between the first
arrival of Satan in Paradise (Book IV) and the Fall
(Book IX) there is a pause. Books V and VI, however,
are largely taken up by Raphael's account of the war
in heaven, and therefore, effectively, the pause is
postponed to the Seventh Book where he recounts
the Creation, and the Eighth where Adam describes
his own waking and meeting with Eve. But they are
preceded by the lovely appearance of the Archangel

and his first talk with Adam, and the war is told
by him and not directly by Milton; so that even that
strife is a little removed. It is all around Eden, but
it is not within. Satan and the agonizing double
consciousness are postponed. In so far as Milton's
poetry could be tender and gentle and at peace—
and that was much more than is often admitted—it
is so here. Here is Adam's great speech on Eve—
though Raphael does a little grudge it him; here is
Raphael's own definition of free will—'We freely
love'. He says it, and for a moment a sudden new
universe hovers in *Paradise Lost*; he says it, and goes
on to speak of the war. Nothing like it happened
again in Milton—except (almost) when Adam ate
the fruit that he might not be parted from Eve, and
(quite) when Eve offered herself as a just victim for
Adam's fault as well as hers.

'We freely love.' Perhaps 'the affable Archangel'
did not notice the high perfection of the phrase. It
—and it alone—is the complete and final answer to
Satan's spoken taunts and Adam's perplexities; the
following books are a kind of descant on it. But it was
not to be explored, and, unexplored, it is not sufficiently related to the greatness and complexity of
Satan to be a progress from him. And when we come
to the Fall and what follows, we find that we are
returning towards a variation on the earlier theme of
union in division.

The duplication of this state in Adam occupies,
with its results, the last part of *Paradise Lost*. But
there is a difference: in Satan his past and future are
subordinated by the manner of the poetry to his own
intense immediate being; in Adam the immediate

being is subordinated to his past and future. Adam
is largely concerned with what will happen to him and
to his sons, unrealized as yet, whereas Satan seems
to have realized and accepted his future. Adam's
looming future, both of despair and grace, is a great
poetic fact, but it is a fact of inquiry, uncertainty,
and dread, not of finality. Besides which, Adam
argues, and when a poet's character argues it is
always possible to disagree. With the speech in which
Adam proves to his own satisfaction that he must not
regard God as responsible it is not only possible
but necessary to disagree. This however passes,
and there follows the vision of the future which
occupies Books XI and XII. Passages of this, and
the art of Milton through the whole of it, one can
enjoy; but as a vision it is perhaps something of an
anti-climax. Even Milton seems to have tired. He
had formerly used all sorts of phrases to describe an
Angel speaking—'the Angelic Virtue answered
mild', 'Raphael . . . benevolent and facile thus
replied', 'So spake the godlike power', 'Thus he in
scorn', 'which Gabriel spying thus bespake', and so
on. He now used 'To whom thus Michael' (or 'the
Archangel') eleven times, and for the rest only
'said' or 'answered Michael': indeed at one point,
when the two are discussing

> Convulsions, epilepsies, fierce catarrhs,
> Intestine stone and ulcer, colic pangs,
> Dropsies, and asthmas, and joint-racking rheums

(and how dreadful the threat of the verse is!), and
Adam asks if there is any escape—at this point
Milton for a moment seems to give up the effort—

> There is, said Michael, if thou well observe
> The rule of not too much.

But he recovered himself for the serene and terrible close. Amid vision and prophecy, amid suggested capacities of good and evil, amid counsels meant to direct prolonged life, *Paradise Lost* ends; it ends in suspense, in banishment, in journeying, in expectation, in hope. It ends with the departure from that gate 'with dreadful faces thronged and fiery arms' of 'our lingering parents'; but not the least of those dreadful faces was the one which Milton's genius had sealed with the knowledge of unutterable division and the union of immortal and irreconcilable states; not the least of the angelic voices was that which uttered

> Hail, horrors, hail,
> Infernal world, and thou, profoundest hell,
> Receive thy new possessor.

II

The third answer is *Samson*, but another poem came between. *Paradise Regained*, by general consent, is not so great a poem as *Paradise Lost*. The general consent may partly be due to the fact that an argument is less interesting than a story, especially a story where the exciting parts are as exciting as Milton made them. In the first poem Milton improved to such an extent on the few hints which the Bible gave him that we have all attributed Biblical authority to his work ever since, so final has it seemed. But the Temptation of Christ is much more exciting in the Bible than it is in Milton. The short anecdote which opens with the apocalyptic figure of the newly baptized God 'driven up by the Spirit into the wilderness to be tempted of the devil' has a concentrated force which is dispelled even by such a stately loveliness as

> So spake our Morning Star, then in his rise.

and which is not recovered till we come to

> To whom thus Jesus: Also it is written,
> Tempt not the Lord thy God, he said and stood,
> But Satan smitten with amazement fell.

We have of course to remember that Satan is not merely trying to tempt God; he is trying to find out whether it is God whom he is tempting, and the temptation itself is the only means of doing so. 'Who this is we must learn.' It is this inquiry which he pursues throughout up to that sudden great moment at which he at last discovers in his opponent's nature, not in his words, the actual truth:

> As that Theban monster that proposed
> Her riddle, and him, who solved it not, devoured;
> That once found out and solved, for grief and spite
> Cast herself headlong from th' Ismenian steep,
> So strook with dread and anguish fell the fiend.

All his arguments have meant just this, and Christ's answers are adequate—not perhaps always to the argument but—to the purpose behind the argument. He says, in effect, 'Find out what I am if you can; it is not my business to tell you. I shall answer precisely what you ask, and we shall see how much farther on you are.'

It is this underlying conflict which prevents the

dispute from being a purely philosophical discussion, this conflict between Satan's burning anxiety to know, and Christ's contented patience.

What concerns my knowledge God reveals.

It is otherwise a discussion on values. It has a likeness to the discussion of values by the Trojan princes, to Wordsworth's concern with

> the ground
> Of obligation, what the rule and whence
> The sanction.

Shakespeare abandoned his discussion; Wordsworth abandoned his ('yielded up moral questions in despair'); Milton, closing his in a stately decency, nevertheless abandoned it also. Christ, in a sudden burst of energetic poetry, stands; the devil falls in 'amazement'. Something new has entered the discussion and destroyed it. The style of that discussion is —with reverence be it spoken—less compelling than that of *Paradise Lost*; i.e. it is possible, almost anywhere, to stop reading *Paradise Regained* whereas it is almost impossible to stop reading *Paradise Lost*, once one has begun. This may be why comparatively few people begin.

Whether as a result of this changed concern or not, it is to be noticed that the characters of the later *Paradise* are diminished from their former augustitude. Satan is less, but also Christ is less. The most unfortunate personage, however, is Belial, who was thus originally described:

> Belial, in act more graceful and humane;
> A fairer person lost not heaven; he seemed
> For dignity composed and high exploit.

It is true 'all was false and hollow', for 'his thoughts
were low': still— But he has now become

> Belial the dissolutest spirit that fell,
> The sensuallest, and after Asmodai
> The fleshliest incubus.

'A fairer person'—'the fleshliest incubus'. But of
course he appears in the second *Paradise ad hoc.* He
is there merely to propose tempting Christ by women

> Skill'd . . . to draw
> Hearts after them tangled in amorous nets.

His proposal is scornfully rejected, and the entire
omission of that temptation (remarkable even in the
original, except on the orthodox hypothesis of the
Nature of Christ) explained.[1] The 'Filial Godhead'
and 'the archangel ruined' are both of smaller
appearance and less lonely kind. As there are no
great defiances so there are no great solitaries.
Christ had been more lonely in heaven than he is
on earth, among the angelic choirs than in the wilderness. He is here—if not comfortable—at least not much
more than uncomfortable. He had such thoughts

> as well might recommend
> Such solitude before choicest society.

The Lady in *Comus* perhaps had them also. But
hardly Satan or Abdiel or the later Samson. Their
thoughts might *drive* them to solitude, but that is
not the same thing.

---

[1] It is perhaps worth remarking that one of our greatest difficulties
in the scheme of *Paradise Lost* is to understand why the rebel angels,
except Satan, were ever in heaven at all. Moloch, Mammon, and
Belial, are quite unsuitable to it, and we are not told that their natures
were changed by their fall. However, it is part of the story and must
be accepted as such.

Is then *Paradise Regained* a kind of active pause between *Paradise Lost* and *Samson*? It would hardly please Milton to say so, and indeed (though it has a hint of Milton at his lordly ease about it) it is something more. What more may be found by asking another question—Why the Temptation? Paradise was never regained, according to any Christian dogma or even according to *Paradise Lost,* until the Passion and Resurrection of Christ. Yet Milton proposes to sing

> Recover'd Paradise to all mankind,
> By one man's firm obedience.

Intellectually, theologically, the answer is that the 'firm obedience' of Christ to the Father's will can be presented as well by the Temptation as by the Passion; and it is in such obedience that the virtue of Christ's human will lay. This being so, and the Temptation being (to that extent) a proper subject, it follows (1) that it was in Christ's human will that Milton was interested, (2) that an argument was much more suited to the Temptation than the Passion, (3) that the Passion might easily have involved Milton in a problem far too much like that of Satan in *Paradise Lost* to be desirable.

Properly to discuss the first of these would involve theology. It may be sufficient to say that Milton's aristocratic and hierarchic mind had hardly ever succeeded—except in a descriptive line or two— in identifying the Person of Christ with the Equal Godhead of the Son. The Son is begotten in time by the will of the Father; and throughout the whole first poem he is entirely subordinate. He is the impersonization of the Will accepting the Good, not necessary to the Good. *Paradise Lost* and the Athanasian Creed (which is also a very fine poem) are entirely opposed. Long before, at the time of the Ode on the Nativity, it had been a serious and conscious poem which Milton sent to a serious and conscious Child. A thousand carols had sung of the innocence, the helplessness, of the incarnate Godhead. But Milton, it seems, was incapable of seeing Omnipotence helpless and an infant; it had to be something other than Omnipotence. Could the blank verse which is the sound of that Omnipotence break into the nervous singleness of 'I sing of a Lady'? There could only be Omnipotence, and therefore Christ must be something other. It is his subordinated, his human, will in which we are to be interested.

Besides this, it seems that Milton was going to write a discussion. It is not very likely, whatever his ostensible subject had been, that he would have done anything else, since that is what he *did* do. He could, obviously, have treated the Temptation in an entirely different way; he need not have made it an argument. Since he did, it must be assumed that he would have made any subject into an argument, and his genius saved him from a less suitable subject. Christ is something of a public character. He recounts (I. 202) how in his childhood all his mind

was set
Serious to learn and know, and thence to do
What might be public good; myself I thought
Born to that end.

He abandons this idea, but still the poem never convincingly expresses salvation. What, in effect, we have is something rather like a devout and aristocratic statesman being interviewed, at the request of the Government, by an atheistical and ungentlemanly newspaper-correspondent, who goes even beyond his limits in recommending policies and means to policies. Now, whatever the figure of the Crucifixion may have been, it was not that of a devout aristocratic statesman. It was a figure in some respects (as Blake saw) much more like the figure of Satan in *Paradise Lost*.

> All is not lost; the unconquerable will,
> And study of revenge, immortal hate,
> And courage never to submit or yield,
> And what is else not to be overcome.

Of those four lines only one is Satan's peculiarly; the others are equally Christ's. Indeed, on the Christian, on Milton's theory, the last is Christ's *only*; for there can be nothing which cannot be overcome except Christ. And God.

'Milton', said Blake, 'was of the devil's party without knowing it.' If this meant that Milton admired his devil more than his Christ it would be silly. But if it means that he had given the whole great striving with the contradiction in things, all the force it has in itself, and all the strength necessary to meet and bear it without yielding to it—that he had given all this to Satan, and could not therefore repeat it with Christ, then Blake was quite right. A poem on the Crucifixion would have been altogether too much like the self-knowledge of the earlier power which dared

> Through all the coasts of dark destruction seek
> Deliverance for us all.

In the Temptation Milton was able to present Christ as submissive; the Crucifixion would have shown him defiant—and not an aristocratic defiance at that, but a much more desperate one, a defiance (so to speak) of the universe by the universe. When the Image of Godhead demanded of Godhead 'Why hast Thou forsaken me?'—what did Milton propose to do about that? Nothing; he did a wiser thing—he waited, and then took a mortal figure, as much less in kind than Satan as Christ would have been more, and gave to Samson defiance and submission, entreaty and protest, before he touched on the mystery of the reconciled self-consciousness of man.

Meanwhile, in *Paradise Regained*, he did two things. (1) He enjoyed himself with a long discussion between a Miltonic intellect and a coarser—say, King Charles II's or the Bishop of London's. (2) He used this to suggest the impossibility of the lesser nature understanding—not merely what the greater one is doing, but what the greater one is. There had been in *Paradise Lost*—amid all the battles and judgements and talk about free will—that marvellous moment when Raphael uttered three words: 'we freely love'. It is no use for any one—angel or mortal—trying to find that out except by doing it. *Paradise Regained* is the effort of Milton's aristocratic intellect to explain to the devil the nature of love and freedom. Milton may make mistakes sometimes in the argument. But that is its basis.

'Do this', Satan suggests, 'that I may know what you are.' 'If I did that,' Christ answers, 'I should be you and not myself.' 'But why won't you do that?' Satan presses. 'Precisely because I am myself and

not you,' Christ answers again. 'I don't understand
you,' Satan exclaims, 'I think you are an obstinate
fool, and I am afraid you are God.' To which Christ
can only add that the devil never could, and never
did, understand God. Farther, Milton could not go;
the human will of Christ was undivided and un-
agonized. It disputed, and triumphed, but it left on
one side the 'conflict of sensations without name'.

The solemn opening of *Samson* does but renew the
movement which had closed *Paradise Lost*. It was
undesirable in discussing that, to have forced its last
two lines into an allusion to the poetry itself; but in
Samson it is another matter. Of the fifteen thousand
or so lines which made up Milton's work there
remained but something under two thousand: seven-
eighths of his journey had been covered. And now,
after that discussion which was *Paradise Regained*,
the movement recommences.

> They hand in hand, with wandring steps and slow,
> Through.Eden took their solitary way.

> A little onward lend thy guiding hand
> To these dark steps, a little further on.

The first of those couplets is narrative; the second
dramatic. It was by God knows what artistic accident
that Milton turned to drama at the end, but it was of
the most profound use; and perhaps the power of his
genius alone dictated it. For in *Samson* almost for the
first time, certainly only for the second time—it
depends on whether we reckon *Comus* as drama—
his poetry chose a form in which its business was, to
an extent, to conceal his art. In the *Paradises* he had
displayed it; the high invocations, the personal

irruptions, had all contributed to make us aware of
the self-consciousness which was part of the poem.
Poetry was never more self-conscious than in the
Paradises, and its self-consciousness is, in a certain
sense, one with its subject. But, as far as he could—
he could not very far—this self-consciousness was
withdrawn in *Samson*; where it was not withdrawn
it was formally conventionalized; and where it could
be neither withdrawn or conventionalized it was
intensified into human emotion. An example of the
first method is to be seen in a comparison between
the two laments over blindness. The first is in
Paradise Lost at the opening of the Third Book:
those noble fifty lines of which the concluding
passage begins—

> Thus with the year
> Seasons return, but not to me returns—

Compare with that Samson's

> O dark, dark, dark, amid the blaze of noon,

and what follows. Neither is more moving than the
other; but the one awakes in us a knowledge of our
capacity for realizing that we are blind; the other a
knowledge of our capacity for blindness. The second
method is the introduction of the Chorus. Now the
Chorus are come

> To visit or bewail thee, or if better,
> Counsel or consolation we may bring,
> Salve to thy sores.

They form the recording, the commenting, the
exhorting or encouraging faculty of the mind; they
are self-awareness personified. It is this which 'bears
witness' to Samson's patriotism, warns him to 'advise

how to receive' Manoah, remembers old stories and
applies them, universalizes Samson's, and sums up
the moral of the whole. A great deal of what the
Chorus says might be uttered by Samson himself.
The rest is that general expansion of self-consciousness beyond his own, into man's, that is, poetry's,
which in the end concludes and consummates the
progress of Milton's genius. Had *Samson* been a
narrative poem the part of the Chorus would have
been divided between the protagonist and the poet:
self-arguments (as with Satan), or adjectives, descrip-
tions, and comments (as from Milton) would have
taken its place. But the dramatic form enabled this
element to be withdrawn from both sources and
united in one utterance.

Of course Samson in himself remains self-conscious; he does not lose in realism because this other
means of speech had been used. The necessity
which perhaps dictated it was the need for some
comment upon the whole of Samson's experience.
But Samson was to die, and even if he had survived
still the self-conscious poetry of Milton must discover
its own finality—something larger than the hero's.

It is perhaps fanciful to see in the irregular metre
of *Samson* a variation on that blank verse of the
Paradise Lost which was so intensely significant of
its Deity. Yet the later rhythms—not more subtle
nor more beautiful—are less triumphantly controlling
everything. They pause; they hesitate; they change.
But so does the earlier blank verse? Yes, but never
without a much more immediate reference to the
norm; in *Samson* we are passing as far as possible
from a universal norm. Indeed in some places the

norm is only reached again with difficulty, if at all.
I leave the discussion to the prosodists; only adding
that the variations of rhythm combine with the
sharpness of direct human experience in the poem to
remove us from the verbal reflection of the ruling
Will. The modulation is not merely stylistic or
dramatic; it is also metaphysical and poetic.

Samson is a solitary figure like the Lady, Satan,
Abdiel, and Christ: the poem is in this sense a
repetition of the earlier poems. But there are three
differences:

(1) Samson's own state of being;
(2) The thrice-recurring dispute with God;
(3) The allusion to 'dire necessity'.

The poetry is not here expressing a spirit capable
of sustaining division and contradiction: it has gone
beyond that. Satan's vital energy kept him from
perishing. But Samson's vital energy is already
perishing. He is perhaps a less tremendous figure
than Satan. But he is in a state of defeat which
Satan never was. The poetry awakens our knowledge
of a more extreme collapse—a collapse as extreme as
a great solitary can consciously suffer and yet consciously still exist. The sense of being overwhelmed
by Omnipotence is in both Satan and Samson.
Satan's answer is 'Evil, be thou my good': his defeat
shall be his life. If he must know himself so, he will
'enjoy' that sole method of knowing himself. But
Samson is expecting to cease to know himself.
Against the earlier 'unconquerable will' we have
a conquered will—or rather a conquered *being*, a
'double darkness'.

<pre>   Nature within me seems
  In all her functions weary of herself;
  My race of glory run,
</pre>

glory of Satan or glory of Christ

<pre>   and race of shame,
  And I shall shortly be with them that rest.

  Nor am I in the list of them that hope;
  Hopeless are all my evils, all remediless;
  This one prayer yet remains, might I be heard,
  No long petition, speedy death,
  The close of all my miseries, and the balm.
</pre>

Adam had thought that this might be the best for all mankind; here is mankind asking for it. But there is a difference. Adam had, so to speak, taken all the blame. Samson once, Manoah once, the Chorus once, question the actions of God. They do it with all reserves; they stop one another doing it; but they do do it. Personal suffering, contemplation of another's suffering, contemplation of the general state of man, all begin to cry out. Man's self-consciousness is bound to admit his common fate—

<pre>   Just or unjust, alike seem miserable,
    For oft alike, both come to evil end.
</pre>

And the poetry itself? What but this poetry which had set out to 'justify the ways of God'—now come to a point where it is rebuking God—exclaims

<pre>   So deal not with this once thy glorious Champion,
    The Image of thy strength, and mighty Minister.
    What do I beg? how hast thou dealt already?
    Behold him in this state calamitous, and turn
    His labours, for thou canst, to peaceful end.
</pre>

'The Image of thy strength, and mighty Minister'—
is there a better description of Milton's work? 'State
calamitous'—is it not when this image of the good
man 'blinded in Gaza at the mill with slaves' is the
best result of justification? Here is the good man
demanding justification. 'Yet why?' says Samson,
even in the midst of blaming himself. God can 'with
his own laws best dispense'; it is he who prompted
Samson 'to seek in marriage that fallacious Bride'.
Again similarly Manoah protests

> Alas methinks whom God hath chosen once
> . . . He should not so o'erwhelm.

> Immeasurable strength they might behold
> In me, of wisdom nothing more than mean;
> This with the other should at least have paired,
> These two proportioned ill drove me transverse.

Similarly the Chorus—in a passage too long to
quote in full (667–704).

It is this bewilderment, even more than any
exterior likeness between Milton and Samson, which
makes that great line applicable to this last poem.
The poetry that was to see and tell 'of things invisible
to mortal sight' was itself blinded; it was in Gaza at
the mill with slaves. But there it found its confession;
in a poem unrelieved by any but mortal defiance of
mortals Milton's poetic mind used a phrase which
Paradise Lost would have had to explain away.
Samson dies; the Chorus, contemplating that death,
exclaim that he is victorious

> Among thy slain self-killed
> Not willingly, but tangled in the fold

Of dire necessity, whose law in death conjoined
Thee with thy slaughtered foes in number more
Than all thy life had slain before.

The words refer directly to the death, but they
carry with them a larger implication; they admit at
long last something which Milton had excluded till
now. Necessity has brought Samson to an unforeseen
end. And what is necessity but God dispensing with
his own laws, and ill-proportioned strength and
wisdom, and all against which protests have been
entered? Victory now is in defeat; defeat in victory;
the champion and the enemies of God are alike
overwhelmed. There is, so far forth, no thought of
Samson in any future life; the Chorus and Manoah
are concerned with two things: (1) Samson's secular
fame, (2) their own awareness of his death. There
flashes into the verse—for the last time—one of those
reminiscences of Shakespeare which had occasionally
occurred in Milton: curiously in an allusion to the
phœnix, to a new life rising from an old, to a
transmutation of beauty and power.[1] And then we
come to the separate awareness which Manoah and
the Chorus have of the death of Samson. Manoah
is concerned with it as a noble fact. 'Nothing is here
for tears'—he will gather the body and build over it
a (very Miltonic) monument. Samson will have his

[1] It is obvious, in fact, as modern criticism does not yet seem
boldly to have said, that these lines are by Shakespeare; it is therefore
obvious that Shakespeare had a hand in *Samson*; and therefore that
Milton was not composing a poem of his own but revising an old
one. An edition of *Samson* assigning the different parts to the
probable authors is much to be desired. Bacon may easily have had a
hand in the political parts and perhaps Jonson in the classical
allusions. Perhaps only the Delilah speech is Milton's.

place in the history and fame of the world, his acts
enrolled in poetry,

> Copious legend or sweet lyric song.

His memory will awake in others the consciousness
of great deeds; it is the business (some hold) of
poetry.

But the Chorus, not denying this, have, however
short their speech, something else to say. They too
are aware that a great reconciliation has taken place;
they have their own knowledge; their knowledge is
Milton; and that knowledge is peace.

Poetry in *Paradise Lost* had consisted of the narrator and the narrative; in *Samson* these are dramatized
into the Chorus and the actors. But *Paradise Lost*
had ended with the emphasis on the narrative;
Samson ends with the emphasis on the Chorus. It is
they who are aware of their own alteration.

> His servants he with new acquist
> Of true experience from this great event,
> With peace and consolation hath dismist,
> And calm of mind all passion spent.

The mind knowing things had always been an
ostensible part of Milton as it had never ostensibly
been of Shakespeare. It is of the mind knowing
things that these words are spoken. Yet—that
allowed—perhaps this conclusion is not so far from
the close of Shakespeare's own verse. It was after
many ways of dealing with life had been discovered
by poetry that the 'great globe itself' vanished, and
the music of Ariel was heard. It is that vanishing
which, in another manner, the more conscious Milton
calls 'all passion spent'.

Milton's genius remained conscious of itself. It could not become other, as Shakespeare's did in the end. It is not possible for Shakespeare's genius to *know* it is being pardon or Ariel; pardon that knows itself is not pardon, Ariel self-conscious of his non-humanity could not be Ariel. Self-consciousness can only be calm.

He had, in the young brightness of the Attendant Spirit, sung long ago

> —If Virtue feeble were,
> Heaven itself would stoop to her.

But not as quickly as all that. Virtue—poetry—had to go elsewhere—

> To-morrow to fresh woods and pastures new.

And still farther after the thing inseparate had been known in Satan—after change, solitude, and action—

> They hand in hand, with wandring steps and slow
> Through Eden took their solitary way.

It prophesied its own secret return to a reconciled knowledge:

> he unobserved
> Home to his mother's house private returned;

and at last to

> calm of mind, all passion spent.

Heaven had stooped to virtue in a very different way from that which the Attendant Spirit may be supposed to have expected. The justification of the ways of God to man had spread as a final calm through the consciousness in which war had ceased by mutual destruction.

The end of *Paradise Lost* in one sense returns to the beginning. Our first parents issue into a world where experiences already impersonated in the poetic figure of Satan await them. Adam's vision has shown them so much. Their solitary way is, as Milton's moral imagination presented it, either Satan's journey through chaos or Abdiel's through a veiled heaven. It leads to Troilus and Othello, to Lear on the heath and Wordsworth in the church. It leads also to *Samson*; where, as Shakespeare had set the concord of two opposites against the discord of two opposites, so Milton set the quiet of the conscious mind beholding a somewhat similar simultaneous defeat and victory. Shakespeare's subject had been things being so—even their knowing themselves had been part of their being. But Milton divided the spirit of man; and so was able to take, in a sense, an even more extreme moment. Poetry in Shakespeare had imagined at one moment death and life. But poetry in Milton imagined that moment as having been and it was composed in itself—'all passion spent'.

The phrase is the self-awareness of that state in which Shakespeare produced the last plays.

V

WORDSWORTH

'FROM Milton', said Landor, 'one must descend, whichever road one takes.' Even to find Shakespeare or find Wordsworth, though then in order to reascend; and of Shakespeare and Wordsworth it is true also. There are other poets of almost equal height, but they are only peaks compared with those three great ranges. There are other ranges, but they are not so high and they are made up of many poets.

To ascend Wordsworth is to ascend a mountain around which there clings a perpetual mist. Often that mist disappears or is blown apart, and then landscapes open below us, landscapes comparable to those we see from Milton or Shakespeare, landscapes of the mind of men. And then the mist gathers again and we are for awhile lost in it. It is this uncertainty gathering over the certainty, this intermission of sight, which is unique in Wordsworth among the three greatest poets. He possesses a power as great in its opening maturity as Milton's, yet that maturity never itself matures; the greatness of his poetry suffers no diminution even when compared with that other sublime sound; yet it moves to no final state of resolution. At its greatest his poetry is as far beyond the capacity of the human voice to utter as either Milton's or Shakespeare's. 'She should have died hereafter' cannot be spoken; it means more than our voice can carry: so does

> Jehovah, who in one night when he passed
> From Egypt, marching.

Our tongues cannot echo that divine exodus; we
feel it as the soldiers felt the music when the god left
the palaces of Alexandria. So with the finest things of
Wordsworth—

> In beauty exalted as it is itself
> In quality and fabric more divine.

> Mighty poets in their misery dead.

> Diversity of strength
> Attends us, if but once we have been strong.

> And O ye Fountains, Meadows, Hills, and Groves,
> Forebode not any severing of our Loves;
> I only have relinquished one delight
> To live beneath your more habitual sway.

The solemn sincerity of such lines is beyond the
compass of our voices. The manner in which
Shakespeare, Milton, and Wordsworth respectively
defeat us would form the subject for another inquiry.
Roughly, it may be suggested that Shakespeare does
it by a unison of many implied if not expressed (but
usually expressed) intellectual as well as emotional
intensities; Milton does it by arousing a sense of the
awful spiritual importance of a particular intensity;
Wordsworth by arousing a sense of the unity of
individual life with universal life. The shell of his
verse 'murmurs of the ocean whence it came';
something more than us, more than Wordsworth,
more than the poetry of Wordsworth, seems to
open up and expand in the sound, as afterwards it
withdraws and closes itself in the more expected,
but still noble, verse to which it returns. Those
central successes in all poets dispose themselves
through the rest of the verse, which approaches or

recedes from them, and is affected by them. But Wordsworth's style is more dangerous than Milton's. Milton's includes everything in its godlike capacity; if we protest and rebel, we are hurled headlong from that ethereal sky. But Wordsworth's is natural and has the dangers of nature. It is diffused; we do not escape from it—or from nature—so easily as we think. A page even of the worst part of the *Excursion* has often something attractive about it. The details Wordsworth inserts are there because they were there or would be there in nature, and Wordsworth is reluctant to leave anything out. But we are more easily tired.

At its greatest, this is his poetry. But there is, not merely the rest of it but, the depressing rest of it. Of course, he wrote badly sometimes; that is nothing. Shakespeare did it so often that we have—some of us —almost had to rob him of most of his work. Milton did it sometimes; a personal confession may admit that a few lines at the end of *Samson* (of all places in poetry!) appear almost funny:

His lot unfortunate in nuptial choice,
From whence captivity and loss of eyes.

Even the 'tame villatic fowl', just previously? I do not myself find the explanation of angelic digestion funny, and the use of artillery seems just an intellectual mistake, like the temporal begetting of the Son. But however this may be, even Milton occasionally lost hold. These poetic failures do not count. We can excuse, we can even enjoy, such a break as

'Impute it not to impatience, if', exclaimed
The Wanderer, ' I infer that he was healed
By perseverance in the course prescribed'.

It should never be imputed to our impatience that we over-zealously protested against such things; nor against 'Spade! with which Wilkinson hath tilled his land', or 'then cheered by short refreshment, sallied forth'. But what generations of readers have protested against is the appearance of something in Wordsworth which sounds like poetry and is not poetry, of something neither richly good nor richly bad; in two words, of dull verbiage.

> And shall the venerable halls ye fill
> Refuse to echo the sublime decree?

Who cares? 'Life', Wordsworth had told us, 'is energy of love'; what we need is the corresponding poetic energy.

That he wrote so much when that energy was lacking suggests that he did not recognize his want of it. On the other hand, he never completed the philosophical poem which he purposed, which the *Prelude* was to have preluded, of which the *Excursion* was to have been the second part, and the *Recluse* an extract from the first. The *Excursion* itself is a poem from which poetic energy can be sensibly understood to depart. There are great and noble things in it, as there were scattered through all Wordsworth's later life; and it has a right to demand—what it is not always allowed—that it should be a poem of its own kind and not of ours. But when we have done our best, it remains true that though the *Excursion* has nobler poetry in it than *Don Juan* has, yet *Don Juan* is a better poem and more homogeneous poetry than the *Excursion*. It would be a saint, a 'holy fool' of poetry, who would consent to keep the *Excursion*

and lose *Don Juan*. And his sanctity and his folly
would be equal.

This mass of unsuccessful stuff, this slow change
in the *Excursion*, this abandonment of the great poem
which Wordsworth had intended—to what cause are
they due? to what cause in his poetry, not in his
personal life (with which this essay is not concerned)?
The answer is that his poetry could not sufficiently
trust itself.[1]

Wordsworth had one poetic habit in common with
Milton—the habit of introducing solitary figures.
But there is a difference between them: Milton's
are active, Wordsworth's are passive. Milton's are
in revolt; Wordsworth's are in—what are they in?
They are not in revolt; they are not entirely in
acceptance, at least they are not in willing and exalted
acceptance. They express—or some of them do—
a trust in God. But this is secondary, even where it
occurs, and it does not always occur. They communicate a strange sensation of semi-mystical fear; they
rise before us in that verse, as shapes partly of terror,
partly of sympathy, wholly of mystery. Examples
are the soldier at the end of Book IV of the *Prelude*;
the beggar in Book VII (ll. 635–49); the girl in
Book XII (ll. 248–61); 'the single sheep, and the one

---

[1] To say that Wordsworth did not trust it is hardly sufficient. A
man cannot write poetry by willing it. Besides which, we have no
right to dogmatize about Wordsworth's personal mind. And besides
which again, the very fact that he wrote so much suggests that he
meant to trust, and thought he was trusting, in it. It was his genius
that misled him, not he who miscompelled his genius. But of course
that misleading was partly due to mortal things. I prefer myself
to think that his genius was right in the account which it gave of the
whole matter itself. For these reasons I have not discussed Annette.

blasted tree' also in Book XII (ll. 292–302, 317–
23); the Leech-Gatherer; Margaret (in the *Affliction
of Margaret*—though here the solitary figure speaks);
the old Cumberland Beggar; the Solitary Reaper.
These are the most striking among many solitudes;
there are many others of less apparent significance
—Lucy Gray is one—whose ghost

> sings a solitary song
> That whistles in the wind;

Margaret in the First Book of the *Excursion*, and
other figures scattered through that poem; the
Shepherd at the end of *Michael*; Leonard in the
Brothers; the Forsaken Indian Woman; Ruth—all
these, and more, sing their own solitary songs or
preserve their solitary silences. And around them
is that third circle which is only by accident solitary
—the flowers and birds whom Wordsworth names
singly, the Skylark, the Daisy, the Lesser Celandine,
the Swan on still Saint Mary's lake, the Linnet, the
Butterfly. Add the solitude of Lucy and the recurrent
solitude of Wordsworth himself, and the groups will
be sufficiently presented. Now among these there are,
of course, many human solitaries, many who have
been made lonely by their own actions or those of
others, and this the poems tell us, arousing in us a
sense of our own capacity for solitude and endurance.
It is such things as those that make part of Wordsworth's greatness, confirming his instinctive claim
to be part of our philosophic mind. Michael by the
sheepfold, and Leonard and the Indian Woman, and
Wordsworth, are all presentations of humanity. But
that first group are not in fact presentations of

humanity at all; they are something vaster and
stranger.

Of the London beggar Wordsworth says that his
own 'mind turned round as with the might of waters',

> And on the shape of that unmoving man,
> His steadfast face and sightless eyes, I gazed
> As if admonished from another world.

Of the soldier—or just before—he says, speaking
of Solitude, that by night

> the soul of that great Power is met,
> Sometimes embodied on a public road,

and it is only after 'subduing my heart's specious
cowardice' that he dares speak to that appearance

>   —Companionless
> No dog attending, by no staff sustained,
> He stood
>   his form
> Kept the same awful steadiness—at his feet
> His shadow lay, and moved not.

These are unnerving apparitions—at least, they
almost unnerved Wordsworth; they came to him like
the incarnations of the otherness he had in childhood
known more vaguely in the 'low breathings', or the
peak which called up

> huge and mighty forms that do not live
> Like living men.

And greater than beggar or soldier is the Leech-
Gatherer. Wordsworth gave that poem a second
title—'Resolution and Independence'. It is very
proper that we should read it as, apparently, he meant
us to; it is proper that we should realize what a great

and moving poem it is. But it is permissible also that we should derive from it all that it contains; and one of the things it does contain is a sense that the Leech-Gatherer is the impersonated thought of some other state of being, which the acceptance of the noble doctrine it teaches leaves in itself unexplored.

He seems 'the oldest man . . . that ever wore grey hairs'; he was like 'a huge stone . . . on the bald top of an eminence', that seems 'a thing endowed with sense'; again he was like a

> sea-beast, that on a shelf
> Of rock or sand reposeth, there to sun itself.

He is 'motionless as a cloud that heareth not the loud winds'. He speaks 'in solemn order'—'a lofty utterance'.

> His voice to me was like a stream
> Scarce heard; nor word from word could I divide.
> And the whole body of the man did seem
> Like one whom I had met with in a dream.

His shape, his speech, 'the lonely place', all trouble Wordsworth.

> In my mind's eye I seemed to see him pace
> About the weary moors continually,
> Wandering about alone and silently.

Confronted with this great experience Wordsworth might have done one of two things—in doing the very thing he did do. He asked him, out of the midst of his own bother about his future income— and God, He knows how real and urgent that bother can be; we shall never understand the poets if we pretend that money is not of high importance—he

asked him, 'How is it that you live, and what is it you
do?' And—as if 'sent To give me human strength'—
the Leech-Gatherer told him, and Wordsworth
listened and admired and believed and went away
comforted. Nevertheless, that question might have
been asked with another meaning—with the desire
for some knowledge similar to that which caused
Jacob to wrestle with the Angel: 'What is thy
name?' It might have been asked not for strength
and comfort, but for discovery and increase of poetic
wisdom.

What *is* this apparition—this stone—this sea-
beast—this cloud—this dream-like body—this undivided stream of lofty utterance? What is it in
itself? Never mind what it means to our lives, what
moral or message it has for us, or let that be secondary;
'what is thy *name*?' He belongs to that strange
world from which the woman came, who bore a
pitcher on her head and walked leaning against the
wind, and the beggar who wore a label that seemed

> to typify the utmost we can know
> Both of ourselves and of the universe;

and the soldier who was an embodiment of the power
of Solitude; and the Highland Reaper who sang
'the melancholy song', 'the plaintive numbers', of
which Wordsworth knew that they might be 'of old
unhappy far-off things'.

Lear on the heath, Satan on Niphates—if these
had not been forced by the poets to speak, and speaking, to explain their being, would not they too have
seemed to belong to that terrifying world?

In effect they do. Wordsworth drew from figures

looming as Lear and Satan loomed, as Othello, and the Ghost of Caesar, and Samson in Gaza, a high and lofty doctrine. But it was a doctrine: his poetry ceased to inquire into them; perhaps therefore inevitably his poetry ceased. For it was a doctrine that concerned itself more with the way men should live than with poetry itself.

But so did Milton? *Nego*; at least not before his poetry had done all it could with Satan. Milton trusted poetry absolutely—Satan is the proof— and he was justified. Shakespeare trusted poetry absolutely—Lear and Macbeth are the proofs— and he was justified. But Wordsworth did not, could not, quite do that; therefore his poetry left his philosophy to get on as best it could, and his philosophy could not get on. The great philosophical poem was never written.

I do not suggest that either Milton or Shakespeare put it like that to themselves. But it is clear that both of them did wholly what they had to do, and left the rest to the Muse. It was, after all, *Milton* who dared the sublime defiance of 'Evil, be thou my good'; he himself must have trusted poetry profoundly before he could believe that his poem would get over that. He did not refuse it because his intelligence told him that it might prove harmful or shocking or wrong, just as he did not do it because it was harmful or shocking or wrong. It was Satan. Now there is a sense in which Wordsworth was compelled to avoid his own Solitaries. It is a sense so rare that, though he did it, Wordsworth remains our third greatest poet. But it is a sense so definite that he came near to thinking that good intentions would write poetry for him. It is a sense so unimportant that what he did is still 'felt in the blood and felt along the heart'. But it is a sense so important that what he did is thought to be good for the young and is consistently misapprehended and disliked by the young.[1]

And yet Wordsworth was a very great poet; if he had not been we should not even have known that he missed the final wrestling. It is not to any slackness on his part that we dare attribute this last —this very last—lack. It is to be attributed, little though they knew it, to Pitt and all those who declared war on the Revolution. Or so his poetry states, and what his poetry dared not or did not state must be left to students of his individual life.

The crisis of Troilus and the crisis of Satan is related to the crisis which fell on Wordsworth: at least as he discovers and expresses it in the *Prelude*. There is not only the account itself—'pity and shame', 'change and subversion', a shock 'to my moral nature', 'a revolution, at this one time', 'a stride Into another region', 'from that pleasant station torn And tossed about in whirlwind', 'a conflict of sensations without name'. These are the direct phrases—I do not see how they could be stronger. But there is more—he exulted when Englishmen were defeated, killed, and put to flight. And there follows the picture of Wordsworth, who

[1] There are no doubt exceptions. But any one who has spoken of Wordsworth to the young will know how dull they suppose him to be. Well, of course, as long as we send them to him to discover moral impulses—and at that probably our own—in vernal woods, what can we expect? Bliss is it in *that* dawn to be alive?

loved the village and its people, and its people in the
church at common prayer, himself sitting in the
church, 'like an uninvited guest', silent, feeding 'on
the day of vengeance yet to come'. The last line has
to be fully felt before the depth of this part of
Wordsworth's poetry can be realized. If any one had
asked him what England had done to 'soil our
mothers' he might have answered, exactly in Troilus'
words, 'nothing at all, unless that this were she'.

But *Troilus* was written half-way through Shakespeare's poetic life; so was *Paradise Lost* in Milton's.
It was the poetic immaturity of Wordsworth's *Even-
ing Walk* and *Descriptive Sketches* which suffered subversion. In 1792 Wordsworth all but became a leader
of the Girondins; in 1793 he received this shock; in
1795–6 he wrote the *Borderers*; in 1797–8 he wrote
the *Lyrical Ballads*, the *Recluse, Peter Bell*; in 1799 he
began the *Prelude,* and ended it in 1805. It covered
the second half of his great ten years; somewhere
about the 1803–6 period he wrote also the *Ode on the
Intimations of Immortality,* and in 1805–6 the *Happy
Warrior.* The important point is that his personal
experiences preceded nearly all his poetry; his poetry
followed his personal experiences. No wonder he
talked about emotion recollected in tranquillity!
And how unwise of us to apply the phrase to any
one but Wordsworth.

For from these dates it is clear that when that
crisis of destiny fell on Wordsworth he could not
attempt to explore it in high poetry, because he did
not, till afterwards, reach high poetry.

It is of course just possible, in the abstract, that
he might, in that state of outraged being, have

destroyed all the unpublished poetry he had up to
then written. It is just possible that as Othello
struck at Desdemona, so Wordsworth struck at
what was dearest to him. Poetry was not guilty as
Othello supposed Desdemona to be. But if the
universe had played him false, he might, for a few
moments, have loved and hated what the universe
and England had given him, and in that insanity
destroyed it. 'Evil, be thou my good.' It is not
likely, but it would be possible with any poet, and
it is barely possible with Wordsworth. But it is
likely that there would have been some trace of it
in Dorothy's journals or elsewhere, and it may fairly
safely be assumed that he did not. Besides, there is
Guilt and Sorrow—but he might have left *that*.

His poetry therefore reflected his life up to then;
his concern with Nature, and with man, his consciousness of that dreadful separation of the thing inseparate, and the means by which he was healed. But
his healing, his recovery, was on the hither side of
that divided universe, not on the yonder. His
poetic genius therefore remained on the hither side.
It knew there was another; it knew there was some
greater resolution of the strife in man's heart. But
it never had the strength to go there.

The abdication of the pure poetic authority in his
verse in favour of some other authority is because it
was by some other authority than the purely poetic
that he was revived. 'Imagination and Taste', is the
title of the last two books of the *Prelude*, 'how
impaired and restored'. They were restored; they
were no more than restored—except for the operative
faculty of discovering themselves in poetry. The

comparison of certain lines in the *Prelude* with the
discussion between the Trojan princes in *Troilus* is
too marked to be neglected. 'What is aught but
as 'tis valued?' What is value?

What the rule and whence
The sanction?

Hector had broken off the discussion, by Shakespeare's choice, either designedly or accidentally,
long before that point had been reached. The end
of the argument there is not decision, but Hector.
The farther search was carried on not by the working
of intellect but by the writing of poetry. It is true
that Wordsworth's great subject was not men acting
and suffering; these serve only as illustrations. His
subject was the mind of man in relation to men, to
the universe, and to God. He was—or would have
been—a philosophical and not a dramatic poet. But
poetry is all one; its glory equal, its majesty co-eternal.
It uses doctrines; it does not obey them. It discovers
ways through chaos; it does not follow them. It sits
brooding on the vast abyss; it does not wait till
the abyss has been delimited—even by Nature and
Dorothy.

It could not do this at that time for Wordsworth,
and for that single reason—he was a poet and he was
not writing poetry. His soul relied on other authori-
ties. His poetry, therefore, when it came to be, did
not sufficiently distinguish between its own authority
and that of other traditions. Towards the end of the
Excursion, Wordsworth really does seem to think
that to mention 'the voice of wisdom whispering
Scripture texts' or Baptism was enough; he thought
those things themselves had authority in themselves.

So they may have, but not in poetry. If poetry is to refer to 'Scripture texts' it must make of them a poetic experience; if poetry is to thrill us with Baptism, it must make Baptism part of its own mythology. Wordsworth assumed that merely to mention seduction would make us disapprove of it; but in poetry this is not so, we must be urged by the poetic force. Poetry has to do all its own work; in return it has all its own authority.

Yet for ten years, and at intervals thereafter, how close to that central subject his poetry lay! how near it seems to be to holding in itself the great awareness of the divided consciousness, and presenting some new resolution of it! It has its doctrine for us, and it has more—it has the continual approach of something greater. There is in it the knowledge of something it cannot quite discover. 'We feel that we are greater than we know', 'Thoughts that lie . . . too deep for tears', 'we will teach them how', 'high instincts', the label on the beggar, the 'brightness' of the Happy Warrior. There are strange and solitary forms appearing, on lonely roads, on moors, in cities; and somehow—as in certain antique legends —the poet never asks quite the right question. Wordsworth took part with Coleridge in the *Lyrical Ballads*, and it is not always noticed that the actual themes of their verse are sometimes close. The Ancient Mariner is kindred to those other apparitions; only *they* could not speak of themselves, but must be challenged. The verse which Coleridge added to the *Ancient Mariner*—and blamed himself for adding—is a Wordsworthian verse translated into Coleridgian. 'He prayeth best who lovest best. . . . But Coleridge was right; it ought not to be there. The *Ancient Mariner* is a tale of a similar crisis—of accident, doom, death, and life-in-death —but it flies between Wordsworth and Shakespeare. It has no reference either to man's enduring mind as Wordsworth has, nor to the hiding-places of the new power as Shakespeare has. It is faerie, and therefore the Mariner is compelled to tell the unrelated story. Had it been human, his embodied power would have had to wait to be challenged. Could that figure which was like a sea-beast sunning itself have held Wordsworth as the Mariner held the Wedding Guest . . . but alas, it was not to be.

Nevertheless, what came to be was a great thing. From the *Borderers* to the *Excursion* there is communicated a sense of the human spirit that does everything but what only Shakespeare did. The earliest long poem after the recovery was the *Borderers*. The *Borderers* is precisely an attempt to present a similar crisis to that through which Wordsworth passed—

> There was a plot,
> A hideous plot against the soul of man.

> A man by pain and thought compelled to live,
> Yet loathing life.

> Suffering is permanent, obscure, and dark,
> And shares the nature of infinity.

> The mind of man, upturned,
> Is in all natures a strange spectacle,
> In some a hideous one.

But there is no suggestion of a resolution. Then

there came the many noble poems 'on man, on nature, and on human life', in which the authority of poetry is everywhere present. Among them are the solitaries who are significant of other things, but also those who awake our own knowledge of mighty endurance.

> The gods approve
> The depth and not the tumult of the soul;

the depth of the soul is shown here in the repose which had been restored to Wordsworth, and which he now searched out. Everywhere it is that to which his genius returns, with counsel, with wisdom, with exalted hope. He explores that state of being, even if he leaves others undetermined. The noblest expression of it—outside the *Prelude*—is the *Intimations of Immortality*. It is a platitude to say that it is not about immortality; it is about his own poetry. It is that which 'hath kept watch o'er man's mortality', which feels the 'fallings from us, vanishings', which in certain rare encounters trembles 'like a guilty thing surprised'. It is this which, after the 'hour Of splendour in the grass, of glory in the flower' has disappeared, is to find 'strength in what remains behind'. But strength in what remains behind is not the strength of Imogen, of Perdita, of Pericles, or of Ariel, nor the knowledge of the Chorus in *Samson*.

In the *Excursion* Wordsworth made an effort— a final effort—to gather everything in. He succeeded in manufacturing four eidola of himself: the Wanderer, who is Wordsworth's idea of the incarnation of his own poetic mind; the Solitary, who is Wordsworth's idea of himself gone wrong; the Vicar, who is Wordsworth's idea of himself ordained, and the narrator, who is just Wordsworth. After the first book or two it is almost impossible to be greatly interested. Yet even there poetry breaks out—of the same kind and concern—

> poor humanity's afflicted will
> Struggling in vain with ruthless destiny.

> The intellectual power, through words and things,
> Went sounding on, a dim and perilous way.

It is the very description of poetry making itself; it is a description of Shakespeare and Milton. It is a way, nevertheless, which Wordsworth's genius did not wholly take: it paused almost at the exact point at which he used the lines. For it was humanity's afflicted will struggling *in vain* of which his poetry was most intensely aware. He shaped the image of man repulsed by destiny, and made it into an everlasting nobility. The *Happy Warrior* is a single poem's vision of something else; but it is the *Ode to Duty*, the end of the *Immortality* Ode, the *Elegiac Stanzas*, and other poems of the kind, including parts of the *Prelude* and the *Excursion*, which do the work. This unique presentation we owe to Wordsworth and to Wordsworth alone. The depressing, the uninteresting, verse is a necessary accident of that achievement; we may not read it, but we ought to realize that it is a condition of what we have and do read, and no more to be regarded in itself than the plot of *Cymbeline* is to be solemnly discussed apart from Imogen and the Dirge. That Wordsworth wrote it is due to the same cause that shaped the particular burden of his great poetry—the fact that he, whose subject was his own experience, did not write poetry while he was undergoing that experience. He could not explore his own crisis by meeting it in poetry. He had to deal with his crisis as it had been resolved by other aids, and those aids and their result his poetry never fully assumed. But if we could be allowed to attribute will and intention to the English Muse, it might seem that she deliberately refrained from visiting her son until his central experience was ended, in order that we might have for our delight that great song of solemn endurance and hope. It is a music which might have accompanied Adam and Eve as they passed from Eden at the close of *Paradise Lost*.

THE CRISIS IN LESSER POETS

IN Shakespeare then we have the poetic mind imagining union in contradiction, and afterwards contradiction in union; and after *that* finding itself capable of imagining essential fact and almost of non-human existence. In Milton we have the poetic mind imagining its knowledge of union in contradiction, and afterwards its knowledge of contradiction in union. In Wordsworth we have the poetic mind imagining union in contradiction, and afterwards a life which had to be lived under the shadow of that contradiction. I do not propose any idea of a development from one state to the other; it is extremely dangerous and undesirable to make patterns in poetry. The histories of literature do it, no doubt justly, certainly inevitably. But the result is too often that the greatness of Pope is hidden because he lived in an 'Age of Prose' or that Byron's closeness to the Augustans is unstressed because he lived in the Romantic Revival.

Byron was, in one thing at least, a typical poet of that age. For he was the extreme example of a conscious Romantic poet—his Laras and his Giaours and his Manfreds and his Childe Harolds and his Byrons show it. He walked among the mountains and the chasms trying to lose his poetic head, until Don Juan—like the Chamois Hunter in Manfred— saved it for him. But though he tried more and lost it less than most of his contemporaries, they were not so unlike him. For the whole movement was

a conscious Romantic Revival—in all perhaps but
Coleridge, and his poetry was the least 'period' of
them all. Coleridge, in the peculiar thrill of his
most Coleridgian poetry, might have happened at
any time. He might have been contemporary with
Shakespeare's songs or Crashaw or Christopher
Smart. That wild unintellectualized song might
have broken out anywhere—as things like it break
out everywhere. There was another Coleridge who
was of his period, and he (like the rest) was conscious
of his Romanticism.

It was of course unavoidable. They were in revolt,
and they knew they were in revolt. Keats was
shockingly silly about the poetry of the eighteenth
century; so was Blake. It is true they were rebelling
against the late eighteenth century, and not against
that great age in its great prime. It was time that
they came, but it is no use pretending that they did
not know they had come. Wordsworth studying his
own poetic mind, Keats turning himself (as Apollo)
into a god, Shelley seeing himself as 'a pard-like spirit,
beautiful and swift', Byron throwing fits at the sight
of his own shadow—all these were very great and
wonderful poets. But they were also consciously
romantic. There has never been a time when poetry
was so strongly aware of being poetry; the Augustans
were simpletons beside that.

The Augustans, indeed, had quite another business—and for our present purpose the Augustans
may be taken to mean Pope. Once Pope had
happened, it was impossible for any Romantic not
to be aware that he was being romantic. The attacks
on Pope were but counterblasts to his own attack

—not on Romanticism, but on a false Romanticism, which everywhere and always closely attends on the true. The Muse—terrified of her own excesses—had already appealed from herself drunk to herself sober: the appeal, the denunciation, concludes the *Dunciad*. 'Beauty is truth, truth beauty'—no doubt. Ever since Keats said it, we have all fallen for it. And after having taken up our cross daily over those lines, we may have some right to believe it. But

> See skulking Truth to her old caverns fled,
> Mountains of casuistry heaped o'er her head,
> Physic from Metaphysic begs defence
> And Metaphysic calls for aid on sense.[1]

Beauty *is* truth—but there is a suggestion of truth in a cavern about the phrase.

Pope's poetry is continuously conducting a war. Milton's poetry took warfare as a theme, but Pope's is fighting—not for religion, not for morals, but for poetry. The number of times he used his genius to conduct a personal quarrel need not blind us to the way in which it fought for its own integrity. The eighteenth century was called by Arnold an Age of Prose; but in Pope we see the defeat of prose. He is the defender of poetry; his couplet excludes prose. It does not invite, it repels and masters the antithesis; it transforms, by its compression and its rhythm, the antithesis into something—even at its most rational —slightly irrational. Poetry had often found in rhyme a delight; here it almost found it a refuge. But it decked that refuge with many felicities, because the refuge itself was passionate. Pope's

---

[1] Peculiarly nowadays.

mind was misled often by a philosophy the silliest
that has ever been expressed in verse, or by personal
quarrels; but his genius was never misled. The whole
of *Adonais* has nothing greater than

> Poets themselves must fall like those they sung;
> Deaf the praised ear and mute the tuneful tongue.

'What oft was thought but ne'er so well expressed.'
We have read *'ne'er so well'* too lightly; it is an
aspiration and intention of the most integral poets.

What then is his poetry doing? It is doing its
duty; there is no more moral poetry in English than
Pope's. It hates the second-rate—false Romanticism,
prosy verse, and Addison. It hates ease and comfort.
It does not certainly pass into the state beyond the
crisis of discovery, beyond the solitude and the
change. It does not seek for the springs of action.
But it is the condition, and the only condition, under
which poetry can go farther; it is the expression of
that condition, a poetic chastity which might have
been the Ithuriel of *Paradise Lost*, touching the
toad 'squat by the ear of Eve'. And what a spear!

Pope's genius defends itself; it defends poetry
—but it does not move. As its concern is with the
outer world about it, so its content is to be what it
already is. The disguised sneer—if it were a conscious sneer; if the Muse were not being ironical at
Pope's expense—in the *Essay on Man* denies any
remoter activity on its own part.

> Hope springs eternal in the human breast;
> Man never is but always to be blest.
> The soul, uneasy and confined from home,
> Rests and expatiates in a life to come.

'Man never is but always to be blest.' But Pope's genius did not look forward to any other blessing than it could, then and there, find. It did not desire anything but what it had. His Ariel is almost as exquisite as Shakespeare's; but it is desperately concerned for Belinda as Shakespeare's never was for Prospero, and it would be very unhappy in the elements to which its inhuman brother was dismissed. The couplet discovered and protected poetry in an Age of Reason, but in order to do that it had to give up something; the 'something evermore about to be'.

But when we turn back to the Romantics, especially to the two younger Romantics, Shelley and Keats, we find that movement is an essential part of their genius. What they talk of, they do. The difference between them—perhaps *the* difference between them —is in the attention they give to that movement and to the distance in which it takes place. In Shelley distance is everywhere; in Keats it is nowhere. Shelley is always avoiding the moment; Keats is always closing with it. To say 'avoiding' implies no derogation; it is the nature of Shelley's poetry to act so. It is poetry—his poetry—because it acts so. It is continually on the brink of the moment that has not yet come off. 'Jam to-morrow and jam yesterday; but never jam to-day': Shelley's poetry is the continual dawn, and never (or rarely) the morning of that to-morrow with its jam. He put it more beautifully, but not (I think) otherwise in his own description—

> It is a dying lamp, a falling shower,
> A breaking billow; even whilst we speak
> Is it not broken?

It is not, of course; that is its exquisite success.

But the reader is himself continuously suspended—
in the sight of

> The loftiest star of unascended heaven,
> Pinnacled far in the intense inane;

or in expectation—

> O wind,
> If winter comes, can spring be far behind?

or in journeying—

> I am borne darkly, fearfully afar;

or in hope—

> Another Athens shall arise;

or in devotion—

> The devotion to something afar
> From the sphere of our sorrow;

or in longing—

> Swift be thine approaching flight,
> Come soon, soon!

and again—

> O come,
> Make once more my heart thy home.

or in defeat—

> The winged words on which my soul *would* pierce
> Into the height of Love's rare universe
> Are chains of lead around its flight of fire.

And so on; there are plenty of other quotations.

There are, of course, other poems. But there are
very few which are not breaking billows that do not
break; and even those often break rather uncertainly.
There is *The Revolt of Islam*—but that is supposed

to be a story, and 'any one who reads it for the
story had better hang himself'. There is the *Cenci*,
which somehow breaks in the wrong place and
leaves one with the impression (for all its pathos)
that one has been reading a poetic version of *The
Girl who Took theWrong Turning*, or at best a rather
dated problem play on 'May a girl kill her father?'
There is *Prometheus* which breaks all over the fourth
act, and only part of it crashes in the divine final
chorus. There is *Swellfoot*—and Swellfoot is one
of the things which show that Shelley might have
closed with solitude and change. Nobody reads
Swellfoot, yet without it we have a rather over-
aerial Shelley. Our own Shelley, no doubt, is the
Shelley of

> And others came—Desires and Adorations,
> Wingèd Persuasions and veiled Destinies—

it doesn't a bit matter which of Keats's poems, if
any, was most like a wingèd Persuasion—but these
most lovely personifications of emotions and abstractions ought to be met by something more earthy.
They were; they were met by the Boars in *Swellfoot*.
    The summary of all this is that in Shelley, more
than in any other English poet but Marlowe, we
have this throbbing expectation, sometimes still,
sometimes in movement, sometimes for a moment
almost satisfied. His poetry is troubled with it.
Pope and Shelley together are the double poetry
made by the English Muse out of that state before
the great crisis of poetry. In neither of them is
genius satisfied with itself. But Pope's is doing its
duty and asks no more. Shelley's asks much more,

it is yearning for its own perfection. It is itself
'an inheritor of unfulfilled renown'. It is full of
'undetermined modes of being'; it pines for 'the
hiding-places of man's power'—but it found the
Adriatic instead.

The aspiration in Marlowe is certainly of a very
different sound from Shelley's: it is a heavy billow
of verse, and it is felt in its gathering and rising,
rather than as a slender wave at the moment before
the fall. But both in the subject of *Tamburlaine* and
Faustus and in certain of his finest lines the desire
for 'something afar' is there. Passionate desire is
itself the subject of those plays, and we are made
aware by them of our own capacity for passionate
desire; there is no comment but its dramatic thwart-
ing. *Edward II* is a less magniloquent but a more
pathetic expression of the same theme; and though
The Jew of Malta is a grotesque farce, the undernote
is that of a sinister and extreme longing. The means
which the four protagonists take in which their
search may be conducted vary—glory or learning
or love or riches. The search is for a satisfaction
which *Tamburlaine* at least realized could not be
gained.

> What is beauty, saith my sufferings, then?
> If all the pens that ever poets held
> Had fed the feeling of their masters' thoughts,
> And every sweetness that inspired their hearts,
> Their minds, and muses on admirèd themes;
> If all the heavenly quintessence they still
> From their immortal flowers of poesy,
> Wherein, as in a mirror, we perceive
> The highest reaches of a human wit;

> If these had made one poem's period,
> And all combined in beauty's worthiness,
> Yet should there hover in their restless heads
> One thought, one grace, one wonder, at the least,
> Which into words no virtue can digest.

That other superb longing moves to a similar extreme:

> Nature that framed us of four elements,
> Warring within our breasts for regimen,
> Doth teach us all to have aspiring minds:
> Our souls, whose faculties can comprehend
> The wondrous architecture of the world:
> And measure every wandering planet's course,
> Still climbing after knowledge infinite,
> And always moving as the restless spheres,
> Will us to wear ourselves and never rest,
> Until we reach the ripest fruit of all,
> That perfect bliss and sole felicity,
> The sweet fruition of an earthly crown.[1]

'Every wandering planet's course'—'the loftiest star of unascended heaven'—it is not merely the astronomical image that unites the two poets. Marlowe's verse, more perhaps than Shelley's, is aware of catastrophe; and that for three reasons (*a*) Shelley imported into his longing something moral; he desired perfection—of love and liberty—and he believed that the universe ought to supply it. (*b*) Marlowe had a more intense vision of death—with a love of more spectacular effects he could not resist the most spectacular of all effects. Death fearfully

---

[1] The last line is to us, perhaps, a little of an anticlimax. Crowns are no longer marvellous and symbolical things. But to Marlowe they were magnificent beyond their own scope, and we lose understanding if we lose the imagination of royalty.

stealing round the throne of Asia, or coming to
Faustus amid devils and despairing cries, or trampling
on Edward in his dungeon, or grotesquely torment-
ing Barabbas in the boiling cauldron—all these
shows are great with a fatality which the genius of
Shelley could not admit. (*c*) He realized that when
everything is said there is something that cannot
be said, when everything is gained there is something beyond 'the highest reaches of a human wit'.
Desire in his verse is troubled 'with conceit of foil'.
He was aware of man's limitation. Yet more almost
than any other English poet at the beginning of his
career he was already aware of man's power—

> Our souls whose faculties can comprehend
> The wondrous architecture of the world.

Two words in that first line were used again
by Wordsworth—

> the soul
> Remembering *how* she felt, but what she felt
> Remembering not, retains an obscure sense
> Of possible sublimity, whereto
> With growing faculties she doth aspire.

The sublimity is not far from the wondrous
architecture; only 'architecture' is the more definite
word—sublimity is the sense aroused by the architecture. The earlier word is the strength of its own
line. But it is also the strength with which the
poetic mind explores itself; it is the determination
to discover *what* she felt as well as *how*. The faculties
of the soul in the earlier poem are certain of doing
that which in the later they are beginning to do.
There is not merely aspiration in Marlowe; there is

knowledge. He was already an adult poet. That maturity is in much of his verse; he sent through all our modern poetry the question it seeks to answer

> What is beauty, saith my sufferings, then?

It was taken up, almost exactly two centuries after, by Keats. Excluding Shakespeare and Milton, so great a richness was not felt again until 1820. And Keats?

> Away! away! for I will fly to thee,
>   Not charioted by Bacchus and his pards,
> But on the viewless wings of Poesy,
>   Though the dull brain perplexes and retards:
> Already with thee!

He always was; his future tenses are more immediate than Shelley's present tenses. There has been so much written about Keats of late that it would be superfluous to add much more. It is enough to indicate how Keats was always closing with the moment. In him the distance has been left behind; it is between him and 'the little town' to which none will e'er return. It is abolished by the 'Already with thee!' For the 'Can Spring be far behind?' he has only

> Where are the songs of Spring? Ay, where are they?
> Think not of them; thou hast thy music too.

This capacity of closing with the moment, this intensity of apprehension, received many opportunities. There is very little sign that Keats would ever have been a great dramatic poet. He had been writing a good deal about himself, and in the second *Hyperion* he was writing about himself even more directly than in the first. His poetry is not, in the ordinary sense of the word, philosophical poetry. But in the 1820 volume it does seem in certain places as if his poetry apprehended philosophical change as it had apprehended the love of Isabella or the supper of Madeleine (which she did not stay to taste —Keats had tasted it enough in describing it; he had had his moment and abandoned it). There are five poems particularly in which it was concerning itself with some enlarged state of being. The change was in him known—so urgent was his genius— chiefly by that which is to come after the change. The *Ode on a Grecian Urn* and the *Ode to Psyche* are the preludes; the close of the *Hyperion* is the change symbolized; the *Melancholy* is its moral principle. But the *Nightingale* is the change itself. Nowhere is philosophy less intellectual and more sensational, yet if the sixth and seventh stanzas are not philosophical change known by the poetic mind, it is hard to see what they are indeed about. The movement is announced, in so many words, to be a *poetic* move-ment; and when the book, which we yet await, on poetic logic is written, this poem will be one of the most important texts. The night—the moon and stars—no moon, no stars—'embalmed darkness'— 'darkling I listen'—'easeful Death'—'rich to die'.

But after that death it is the circumstances that have changed; it is then, and not before, that the Nightingale has become archetypal; its song is known after a different manner. Time and place, legend and faerie, are carried on it. The personal death and the archetypal life are supposed to be imagined, even in the poem; that is, the change is not, even there, final. It is rather prophecy than actuality. But it is poetry knowing itself after an everlasting manner. In the last stanza the accident of a word breaks the philosophic trance, and the individual being, the 'sole self' returns. The high state of union fades with the song of the actual bird; imagination of the new life will not provide that life. But the premonitory knowledge was there, and the poem ends with the question of all such initiations: Which is real—that or this? 'Do I wake or sleep?'

In the *Ode to Melancholy* there is the moral principle—especially in the last six lines. The contemplation of poetry is to be of that state where the very temple of Delight and the sovran shrine of Melancholy are one: as Apollo cries to Mnemosyne,

> Creations and destroyings all at once
> Pour into the wide hollows of my brain,
> And deify me.

Perhaps the creation of destruction is the poet's approach, as the tragedies of Shakespeare were his approach, to his final developments. Not because life teaches the poet tragic facts, but because his genius can only grow by discovering tragedy, do the great masters of it turn to that 'sovran shrine'; and then no more like the young Wordsworth with his widow or the young Shakespeare with his Romeo or the young Milton with his escaping Pagan deities, but with the mature Wordsworth and Lear and Satan. It seems 'rich to die', but that was (so the poem says) 'fancy'. When the change took place in the god 'Apollo shriek'd'. The actual richness of dying comes perhaps only after many deaths, from Hamlet to Lear.

It is the subject—in subversion, solitude, change
and expectation of change—of both *Hyperions*.

The other two poems are more remote from the
centre, yet, one by vision, one by worship, they deal
with it. The *Ode to Psyche* invokes it; the *Ode to the
Grecian Urn* contemplates a 'silent form', a 'cold
pastoral', that nevertheless teases us out of thought
to some state where poetry cannot leave its song.
It may be that poetry as much as love leaves, in the
lesser places, 'a heart high sorrowful and cloy'd'.
It does with voluptuous readers; perhaps it does even
with voluptuous writers.

The other great romantic poet, Blake, came under
the sweet, but dangerous, irony of the Muse. The
poet who denounced Reason has been schematized
and tabulated; he exclaimed that 'energy is eternal
delight' and his own has proved an everlasting
puzzle. Few English poets have turned out to be
more hortatory; those that do have been intentionally
and clearly so, whereas Blake's sermons are (as such)
unintentional and obscure. It is impossible to read
the Prophetic Books without delight and continual
expectation of delight—on every page there is something thrilling. But it is also impossible to read them
with anything but a spasmodic interest. The things
that happen are sometimes quite exciting—the
building of Golgonooza or Milton's exodus from the
heavens of Albion or the birth of Orc. The maxims,
counsels, and gospel offered us are obviously of high
moral concern. But the people—the personages,
rather—it is they in whom it is impossible to
be interested. Few readers since Blake himself
can feel any immediate satisfaction in the quarrel

between Palamabron and Rintrah. The destruction of mystery (in *The Four Zoas*) is a moving and wonderful piece of work, but who cares that it was Tharmas who caused it? The reconciliation of Mary and Joseph (in *Jerusalem*) is tremendous, but *Jerusalem* is so much less interesting.

Yet that power of awakening our capacity for seeing sanctity and innocence, and for seeing terror and anger, which was shown in the *Songs of Innocence and of Experience*, was with Blake to the end. Yet he continually proclaimed that pardon which Shakespeare had shown and hardly named. He saw heaven unruined; he saw heaven ruined. He had a clear idea of what was necessary for its restoration. What then did he lack?

He lacked just the union of innocence and experience; he lacked especially a convincing single figure to express it. The orifice between innocence and experience was in him so wide poetically that Ariachne's whole woof would go through; they were 'divided wider than the sky and earth' but they were not at the same time 'inseparate'. There are times when one feels that it is almost going to happen— in *The Everlasting Gospel*, in certain incidents connected with Los and Albion, in *The Ghost of Abel*. Los is so attractive that he is very nearly a real poetic figure, but incarnation of that kind never quite happens. With so much genius on Blake's side and so much goodwill on ours, it seems a pity that we are not absolutely taken up by such a crisis as

Cambridge and Oxford and London
Are driven among the starry wheels, rent away and dissipated
In chasms and abysses of sorrow, enlarged without dimension,
    terrible.

Albion's mountains run with blood; the cries of war and of
  tumult
Resound into the unbounded night; every human perfection
Of mountain and river and city are small and wither'd and
  darken'd.
Cam is a little stream! Ely is almost swallow'd up!
Lincoln and Norwich stand trembling on the brink of
  Udan-Adan!

But— It is not that we have no associations with
Udan-Adan; it is that Blake expects us to have.

Blake's poetry, then, fails for the only reason that
poetry of such great quality can ever fail—because it
is too much concerned with something other than
itself. In his case, it is too much concerned with
morality. He will not stop to make his mythical
figures important because their conduct, their 'criticism of life', is to him so much more important. They
have therefore no depth; they have not the 'hard
black line' for which he clamoured. They are
vapours; therefore they are not significant, for
significance—to us—mysteriously reposes in detail.
There is not in them 'something evermore about
to be', because anything may be at any moment.
Milton had something of the same difficulty in
making Omnipotence interesting. A maxim of
conduct, whether it be 'follow passion' or 'eschew
passion', stops at that; it cannot have a divided heart.

Against these Romantics the Victorian poets—
at least, the two most famous—reveal a certain lack.
Tennyson and Browning are not felt to be such
great poets as Shelley and Keats were; but there is
more to it than that. They are not felt even to be
such great poets as Tennyson and Browning promised

to be. Their genius never fulfilled itself; it never underwent any poetic change. Tennyson's poetry became the verse of an old man instead of a young man, but the poetry itself did not alter. Browning's poetry became too often the verse of a tired mind—of an overtired mind—instead of an active mind, but it had no growth in itself. *The Idylls of the King* are the negation of change in the one; *The Ring and the Book* is the promise of an unfulfilled change in the other. Many reasons might be invented for this, but that is not our concern. All we have to do is to see, if possible, where actually the poetic mind fumbled its business.

To say that it did is not to underrate the achievements of those two poets. They did wonderful things, but for some reason they did not manage the most wonderful. And this not because they were definitely minor poets—they were not. They were not cut off by a hostile fate, as Shelley and Keats were. They were not preoccupied with the salvation of poetry, as Pope was. They did not avoid subjects which might have given them their opportunity—on the contrary, they each accepted one. And there they stopped. They failed only because they did not succeed; their poetic genius issued from that task apparently unchanged.

It has been suggested that in Shakespeare, in Milton, in Wordsworth, we discover solitude. It would be a simple comment, both on Tennyson and Browning, to say that in them there is no solitude, or very little. What character is there in either of whom we naturally think as being alone, except for the briefest moment? And of those that officially are, what solitude but an exterior solitude is communicated? Where does the verse carry on that poetic search for the centre of man's actions, for his initiative, for his centre, which is to be discerned in the greater masters? Where is the divided 'thing inseparate'? Tennyson's people are always doing things; Browning's people are always saying things. There is a solemn activity in the one, an excited activity in the other. But neither the characters nor the poets are moved by 'man's power'.

Put so, the charge sounds, literally, untrue. There is *Lucretius*, there is *Crossing the Bar*. There are two great moments of profound solitude in *The Ring and the Book*. But by neither poet could the effort be maintained. One way or another they 'funked it'. And if we had not all their early greatness, if we had not those rare moments, we should not bother; we should be content to leave them with their admirable work. They knew so much, only they did not know it in poetry.

Yet what they did know in poetry they knew— up to a point—so well. Tennyson delighting in his arranged localities, Browning delighting in his unarranged crises—and one other thing common to both, a macabre element from which their poetry retired. This is acknowledged in Browning— *Porphyria's Lover*, *Childe Roland*, *The Heretic's Tragedy* are examples—but it is not so often acknowledged in Tennyson. Yet it is there—in the *Kraken* poem, in *Maud*, in the *Palace of Art* ('corpses three months old at noon she saw'), in *The Vision of Sin*, in *St. Simeon Stylites*. It is quite clear that among the enjoyments of Tennyson's genius was that of making our poetic flesh creep. Yet this element practically disappears. It disappears—partly, no doubt, before his moral message, but also before his Art. Tennyson is not so much an awful warning of Art for Morality's sake as of Art for Art's sake. By the time he had come to *In Memoriam* he had fled, exactly like the soul in the *Palace of Art*, from 'horrible nightmares'; his capacity for poetry was proceeding precisely 'to mourn and pray'. Humanly speaking, Tennyson may have been quite right; poetically speaking, he was all wrong—it is proved by the sudden rise of his power in *Lucretius* where, for a moment, he twice or three times let that nightmare vision reappear. He subdued himself to his Art; unfortunately he subdued his poetry to it. The lovely cadences roll on; the lovely pictures appear; his poetic mind has 'purged its guilt'. It had purged its guilt and its terror and its intellect. For the *Idylls of the King* are hampered all through by a lack of poetic intellect. They are muddled and they are afraid—and both in the legend of the Grail. It is a perfectly appalling thought that Tennyson was capable of taking the great and awful story of the Dolorous Blow by which Balin, with the ever-bleeding spear that pierced the heart of Christ, wounded the Keeper of the Grail (and darkness and sterility fell on the land, and the Keeper lay wounded until the coming of the High Prince)—it is an appalling thought that Tennyson was capable of turning this into a casual incident by which Balin uses the Sacred Spear as a jumping-pole. 'He defileth heavenly things with earthly uses', squeaks Pellam: and that is precisely what one is compelled

to say of Tennyson. And even that is not all. For
Tennyson's genius almost got the better of him
when he came to deal with Lancelot. In Lancelot
—as far as Tennyson could do it, and in his own
manner—we have that same contradiction which
existed in Troilus and in Satan. It is known in a
different kind: here it is a moral sense contradicting
a moral sense. Lancelot felt he ought not to love
Guinevere, but he felt that all that was good in him
rose from that love, so that when he tries to separate
the two moralities he goes mad, but in his madness
he beholds the Grail 'pall'd in crimson samite'.

It is not necessary to agree with either morality
in order to see that this is a very high and complex
poetic thought, and deserving of very serious poetic
attention. Lancelot's cry is one of the most real
things in Tennyson—

> In me lived a sin
> So strange, of such a kind, that all of pure,
> Noble, and knightly in me twined and clung
> Round that one sin, until the wholesome flower
> And poisonous grew together, *each as each*,
> Not to be pluck'd asunder.

But it is answered by one of the most formal things
in Tennyson's poetry. Arthur simply denies it.

> Thou errest, Lancelot: never yet
> Could all of true and noble in knight and man
> Twine round one sin, whatever it might be,
> With such a closeness, but apart there grew,
> Save that he were the swine thou spakest of,
> Some root of knighthood and pure nobleness.

After that it is not surprising that Lancelot, for
the rest of the poem, puts in a merely formal appear-

ance. He has no more to do there than has the vision of the High Prince. All the loveliness, all the nobility, all the exquisite art and real sensitiveness which are there cannot make up for the refusal of Tennyson's genius to pursue that contradiction farther. It refused doubtless because it felt its strength not great enough; it could give us the things it had to give—places and groups of figures and lines of perfect beauty. But it could not enter deeply into man's sense of outraged being; it could not pursue Lancelot's mind into the dark places, and therefore it could not discover his reconciliation. It could not search the mystery of the legends in which, by a holy substitution, he became the father of Galahad. There is in the *Idylls* much diffused poetry, and much communication of human experience. But that experience was unrelated; Tennyson's genius never went much farther than its own beginning. The volumes of 1842 are, in effect, that beginning. From then to the *Idylls* and to the end the poetry went hovering over the depth into which it never plunged. A fantastic student might see in Tennyson's last poem a comment on his work. In *Crossing the Bar* he is putting out to sea, and looks forward to seeing his pilot face to face, 'when he has crossed the bar'. But an actual pilot leaves the ship after it has crossed the bar, and the ship goes on without him to other seas. Tennyson's poetic ship stopped with the pilot; it hovered continually just outside the harbour bar. It thought of putting out to sea—to the places where Lancelot agonized and Lucretius maddened and the Kraken of that early poem dwelt. But it never did; it preferred to see its pilot face to face.

Nor is that metaphysical crisis in *The Ring and the Book*, though it very nearly is. It is astonishing that Browning, with his vivid intellect, his curiosity, his poetic capacity, never (so far as I remember) quite achieved this particular thing. Something like it occurs several times—there are hints of it in *Sordello*, and it may be that, in another fifty years, *Sordello* will be regarded as one of Browning's best poems. It is not likely, but it is possible. But even so, it is a young poem, and cannot have the emotional greatness which high poetry demands. Again in *The Return of the Druses*, just before Anael cries out 'Hakeem!' there was an opportunity; in *Andrea Del Sarto*—but that is resigned. Browning was never intellectually lazy, but he was often emotionally lazy. It is true he is also emotionally active, but it is an activity which will not undertake heavier labours. It avoids the last profundity by its pace; it loses the inevitable by its dash as much as Tennyson does by his dignity. The inevitable, in poetry as in life, is neither dashing nor dignified. It has speed; it has certitude—for which dash and dignity are popular substitutions. This business, this activity, is the reason why in Browning one feels that any poem almost might have gone differently, any argument been varied, any monologue been twisted by any chance. The monologues are themselves interlocutions; a Browning character is talking to himself. Rarely does the innermost passion force itself to the surface of the words and rule there in awful power.

Yet if he never quite succeeded—and how angry one feels that so fine a poet did not!—in discovering that 'change and subversion', if he always talked

about it too much for us to have a chance of feeling
it, yet twice in *The Ring and the Book* the agony
was too much, and solitude existed. His poems
up to then had generally been active with men's
activities; but there he gave us the intense secrecy of
thwarted desire. The courage for which he has so
often been praised, the noble gospel which he has
been compelled ignobly to preach, was laid aside.
It had been bravery—it had been, at its best, like
Henry V before Agincourt—it was now very much
more like Abdiel in the camp of Satan, or something
even farther from hope. It had been so once before
in Browning—in *Childe Roland*. Though by accident
Pompilia is justified, Browning warns us again and
again that 'many chaste and noble sister fames . . .
lie strangled'. But since Pompilia was justified, he
leaves her content. At the end of Guido's second
speech, at the end of Caponsacchi's sole utterance,
he shows us a figure, which has almost talked itself
into contentment, suddenly realizing the fact. It is
not quite the contradiction of Troilus, but it is in
the next degree. Guido is accepting death—till the
doomsmen come; and then he knows he does not:

> Who are these you have let descend my stair?
> Ha! their accursed psalm! Lights at the sill? . . .

and so on until the terrified shriek calls on his
murdered wife and dies.

The other close is when Caponsacchi has, for a
few minutes, almost talked himself (how Browning
made artistic use here of his chief difficulty!) into
accepting the death of Pompilia. But that cannot
be described; it must be quoted. It is not the division

of 'the thing inseparate', 'heaven ruining from heaven',
but it *is* the realization that heaven itself cannot be.

> I do but play with an imagined life
> Of who, unfettered by a vow, unblessed
> By the higher call,—since you will have it so,—
> Leads it companioned by the woman there...
> To learn not only by a comet's rush
> But a rose's birth,—not by the grandeur, God—
> But the comfort, Christ. All this, how far away!
> Mere delectation, meet for a minute's dream!—
> Just as a drudging student trims his lamp,
> Opens his Plutarch, puts him in the place
> Of Roman, Grecian; draws the patched gown close,
> Dreams, 'Thus should I fight, save or rule the world!'—
> Then smilingly, contentedly, awakes
> To the old solitary nothingness.
> So I from such communion, pass content . . .
> O great, just, good God! Miserable me!

It would serve no purpose to rush past the English
poets, one by one, examining their relationship to this
essential theme. Done briefly it would not be convincing; it would turn what may be (what I believe
is) a truth into what would certainly be a theory and
might rapidly degenerate into a thesis. 'Change'
is one way or another in many of them, discovered
to differing degrees; 'subversion' is in few. There is
something terribly like it in the last poems of Gerard
Hopkins. Whether Hopkins himself was happy or
not (there seems to have been discussion) is, for
poetry, unimportant. But those sonnets awake our
sense of a capacity for so much suffering that the only
possibility is to 'not choose not to be'. He is one
with Satan; he is not one with Lear, from whom will
is gone. There is profound change and solitude in

Coventry Patmore, profound suffering, but it is not (I think) 'heaven ruining from heaven'. Heaven is not mocking itself; his poetry imagines no 'divided empire'. Greater, therefore, in one sense perhaps, it is yet less universally human because of that acquiescent greatness. His unhappy lover (in the *Victories of Love*) suffers, not with Troilus but with Caponsacchi—by deprivation, but not by living contradiction; and those of the odes of the *Unknown Eros* which deal with similar grief do so with a similar limitation.

There is one other poet to whom, for a special reason, allusion should be made. Arnold, I think, has not yet been sufficiently highly rated as a poet. The things which irritate or bore us have been remembered; the things which silence us, forgotten. Yet—outside the three greatest—if one *had* to choose a single poet for the rest of one's life, there are not many who could rival him. He has one of the noblest rebukes in English to the rash romantic spirit:

> So have I heard the cuckoo's parting cry,
>   From the wet field, through the vext garden-trees,
>   Come with the volleying rain and tossing breeze:
> *The bloom is gone, and with the bloom go I.*

> Too quick despairer, wherefore wilt thou go?

It is not a line that can touch Othello or Wordsworth, or Caponsacchi, but for sorrows short of theirs it is a great challenge. But the immediate point is rather different. There is in Arnold a discovery of solitude which in its full power is his alone and which yet is kindred to other lines scattered through English verse—I mean (to take the greatest example at once) the solitude of the river Oxus at the end of

Sohrab. Coldness, brightness, stars, the moon on waters or on snow, are much in Arnold—the Syrian stars 'with shining eyes', 'the scar'd Ortaean snows', 'cherries serv'd in drifts of snow', the splintered 'silver arrows of the moon', 'cold-bubbling springs', 'moon-silver'd inlets', 'cold-shining lights', the solemn peaks known 'to the stars and the cold lunar beams', the wind, the moon, and the rain round the Church at Brou, Judas on the iceberg, caravans mounting the Indian Caucasus 'of milk snow', cattle plunging 'through deep untrodden banks of snow', the sea 'like a bright girdle furled', the mountain-chalet, and so on: there are plenty of other examples. But the greatest of all is the flowing Oxus:

> But the majestic River floated on,
> Out of the mist and hum of that low land,
> Into the frosty starlight, and there mov'd,
> Rejoicing, through the hush'd Chorasmian waste,
> Under the solitary moon; he flow'd
> Right for the Polar Star, past Orgunjè,
> Brimming, and bright, and large: then sands begin
> To hem his watery march, and dam his streams,
> And split his currents; that for many a league
> The shorn and parcell'd Oxus strains along
> Through beds of sand and matted rushy isles—
> Oxus, forgetting the bright speed he had
> In his high mountain cradle in Pamere,
> A foil'd circuitous wanderer: till at last
> The long'd-for dash of waves is heard, and wide
> His luminous home of waters opens, bright
> And tranquil, from whose floor the new-bath'd stars
> Emerge, and shine upon the Aral Sea.

Arnold is personally in his verse a little too concerned with looking away from these things. He does not seem to know of their kinship to other great lines. He is bothered about faith and doubt and we have been bothered with him. But the Oxus is not flowing towards faith or doubt; it is flowing towards a world where Britomart and the 'bright harness'd Angels' are, and Ithuriel and Shakespeare's Valeria,

> Chaste as the icicle
> That's curdied by the frost from purest snow
> And hangs on Dian's temple,

and those other icicles of Coleridge, 'quietly shining to the quiet moon'. These things are not merely pictures; they have something else in them. They awaken some sort of capacity—for motion, for separation, for solitude, for different life. It may be only a fancy, but I have wondered whether this communication is of the sense which poetry has of its own vigil before its own approaching greatness; whether the Oxus flowing towards the Aral Sea is the same thing as Cortez gazing on the Pacific 'with a wild surmise', and the half-drawn figure of Isabella 'enskied' among the votarists of Saint Clare, and the Lady clad in chastity 'as complete steel', and the heights of the Alps which Wordsworth crossed and, remembering, cried out on Imagination, the awful Power that *then* rose 'from the mind's abyss'.

> Thin, thin, the pleasant human noises grow;
>   And faint the city gleams;
> Rare the lone pastoral huts: marvel not thou!
> The solemn peaks but to the stars are known,
> But to the stars, and the cold lunar beams:
> Alone the sun arises, and alone
>   Spring the great streams.

VII
CONCLUSION

WORDSWORTH asserted that in poetry 'forms
and substances' were recognized 'in flashes
and with glory not their own'. The recognition is
ours; it is our capacity for recognizing them that
is struck awake by the glory which is poetry. And
the 'forms and substances' may very well be the
images and principles of human existence: on the
one side, natural objects, men and their works;
on the other, emotions and ideas. The 'glory' that
accompanies these recognized facts moves our delight
and satisfaction; we take joy in hearing even of ruin,
death, terror, because of the completeness with
which those things strike us.

But there is a difference: 'the two great ends of
liberty and power' at which poetry aims are not
achieved all at once, either by the poets or by their
readers. *The Prelude*, besides being an account of
Wordsworth's personal life, and besides being a
study of the development of the working poetic
genius from its beginning to its entering into its
fuller capacities, may also be a study of a reader's
development. It is he as well as the poet who proceeds from a sense of unknown modes of being to the
search for the hiding-places of man's power. Those
hiding-places are themselves recognized in flashes and
with glory not their own. They are therefore double;
they are the hiding-places of the power and of the
glory. It is this double life which we all of us
recognize in great poetry—the life of the 'forms and

substances' of our common concern, and of the glory
which in poetry attends upon them. Yet the two are
one and indivisible—'it is the glory and the good of
art'.

The theme of these studies has been the passing
of the poetic genius from its earlier states to its
full strength. That genius desires nothing but its
own perfection; if we ask anything else

> We do it wrong, being so majestical,
> To offer it the show of violence.

It achieved its full perfection, perhaps, only once in
our literature, in the late style of Shakespeare. There
only did it reach to utter essentials perfectly, detach-
ing itself from all our approach to them; it returned
to its own elemental nature. That was its extreme
'liberty and power'. But short of that, there is much
greatness, and the poets who have it are those to
whom, like Milton, it is habitual, and those to whom,
like Rossetti, it comes as a recognizable but imper-
manent gift. For it seems to have a will of its own;[1]
it appears suddenly in unexpected places. Very
minor poets will loose a line of that greatness, more
distinguished poets will never quite bring it off.
Hardy was a very distinguished poet, but I doubt if
in the whole of his work there is a line of great poetry;
he was, possibly, a greater poet than Rossetti, yet
Rossetti can get that other note a dozen times, and
the echo of it still more often. For there is an echo
as well as a note; the difficulty nowadays with English
poetry is that there has been so much of the echo, we
are so (unintelligently) habituated to it, that we can

[1] I do not say it has a will of its own; I do not know whether it
has or not.

prolong it without necessarily striking the note. That is the difficulty of all traditions, and authentic sound occasionally passes unheard in the general reverberation of the past. It is only by continual exact attention to the centre that we can keep our ears and minds clear.

Towards that centre the poetic mind has passed by different ways. But a thing common to all the ways has been solitude, and by its increasing capacity to express solitude, change, and action, the increasing strength of the poetry is known. Within the outermost circle are such poems as Morris's *The Proud King*, where the story is told, and the loneliness of the King and his conversion are described—beautifully, but only described. Such poems have neither liberty nor power to go farther, nor do they communicate such virtues to us in sufficient measure for us to understand them. *The Proud King, Marmion, Horatius*, have not in them the sense of 'something evermore about to be'; they do not foretell greatness. They are stories—interesting, delightful stories; all the more interesting and delightful for being told in verse. And with those stories goes much lyric; much verse about nature or the world, descriptive comments on gardens or ball-rooms. It is aware generally of nothing but its own pleasure. Just as almost every poet begins by enjoying himself, so poetry itself, in the widest sense of the word, opens with enjoying itself. But presently we are made aware of a different note; passion is felt, and with and because of passion a sensation of greater things. Intellect comes in—as it entered with the Metaphysicals on the simplicity of Elizabethan lyric.

And in making an anthology of English verse on
this method—proceeding, that is, from lesser poetry
to greater, tracing the increasing explorations of the
poetic mind—it is about here that all poems concerned with 'unknown modes of being' would come:
Romeo's speech; extracts from *Comus* and *Prometheus
Unbound*; Keats's *Eve of Saint Agnes*. And at their
close would go two poems by two all-but-great poets
which would call us back from going farther. It is
not, I think, by accident that Pope and Tennyson
each gave us poetry precisely bidding us—

Know then thyself; presume not God to scan.

Come down, O maid, from yonder mountain heights.

Each in its own way the verse of those two poets
looks back over the earlier province rather than
forward over the later. They are the watershed of
real poetic experience; the minor streams flow one
way, the major streams the other. But it is the other
way that Marlowe and Shelley look out—towards
poetic greatness.

Yet the metaphor is misleading, for though somewhere here is a consciousness of poetry's entrance
upon a different concern, yet its state at this point is
not so much a peak as a city. The activities of man
are continually recognized, always 'with glory not
their own'. Here are 'the singing masons building
roofs of gold'; here is Pippa and many of Chaucer's
figures and the poets themselves when they wrote
about themselves—Tennyson mourning for Arthur
Hallam, Wordsworth on Westminster Bridge, Don
Juan, Sporus 'that mere white curd of ass's milk',
Dryden arguing in verse, and Crashaw dedicating his

martyrdoms, and loves and quarrels—personal or
political—past counting. Here, in short, is everything except that poetry which sets out greatly to
discover, by greatly expressing, 'the wondrous architecture of the world'.

But it is the microcosmic architecture with which
poetry is concerned. It is therefore a discovery of
solitude, and the progress of poetry henceforward
is a progress into solitude. The solitary figures of
Browning, the solitary river of Arnold, are the out-
posts and the border of that realm. There are two
entrances to it, and the first and most direct is Keats
—not in the gaze that takes it in from Darien but in
the closing with the living presence of it in the sound
of the nightingale.

> Thou wast not born for death, immortal Bird!
>   No hungry generations tread thee down;
> The voice I hear this passing night was heard
>   In ancient days by emperor and clown:
> Perhaps the self-same song that found a path
>   Through the sad heart of Ruth, when, sick for home,
> She stood in tears amid the alien corn;
>   The same that oft-times hath
> Charmed magic casements, opening on the foam
>   Of perilous seas, in faery lands forlorn.

'The self-same song that found a path': it has to
find a path not merely to sound in, but to understand, the heart of Ruth; it has to do precisely what
here it does—to discover and express, to *be*, after
its own manner, that sick heart itself, in its complex
or simple fullness and scope. Great poetry, in setting
out its own tasks, is always achieving them.

Keats himself, in that poem, was for a little 'tolled

back' to his personal life by the word 'forlorn'. But
poetry has to follow another bell, as if it were that
one which, between the golden-winged Cherub Contemplation and the unsphered spirit of Plato,
sounded—

> Over some wide-watered shore
> Swinging slow with sullen roar.

To the bell which tolled Keats back and that which
called to Milton may be added a third, of which
Ariel sang—'sea-nymphs hourly sing his knell'.
There indeed the 'sole self' is lost for ever; of its
bones are coral made.

But another world has to be passed first, where
Milton outwatched the Bear, 'with thrice-great
Hermes', where (so he instructed us) is philosophy
which knows

> what vast regions hold
> The immortal mind that hath forsook
> Her mansion in this fleshly nook,

and the elemental daemons, and tragedy—Thebes,
Pelops, Troy, and later poets' ennobling thoughts.

The accident of an image connects those worlds;
the accident of another image presents them in
another form. 'If', wrote Shelley, when he was
imagining human perfection and liberty under the
shape of the chained and freed Prometheus—

> if the abyss
> Could utter forth its secrets—But a voice
> Is wanting, the deep truth is imageless.

Imageless, then, for Demogorgon, who speaks, is
like Wordsworth's peak, an 'awful darkness'. The
salvation of Prometheus is touched a little by miracle,

by the undefined magic with the aid of which Sabrina
released the Lady from her chair. Milton had not
then invoked that Spirit who

> Dove-like sat'st brooding on the vast abyss
> And mad'st it pregnant.

From that abyss were to arise Adam and Abdiel
and Christ and Satan and Samson. Wordsworth—
having in poetry crossed the Alps—was halted by
the vision of Imagination itself rising 'from the
mind's abyss'. It is then that he breaks out

> Our destiny, our being's heart and home,
> Is with infinitude and only there.

In another poem he speaks of infinity again—

> Action is transitory—a step, a blow . . .
> Suffering is permanent, obscure and dark,
> And shares the nature of infinity.

This is the difference between Henry V and
Brutus; and the world of Brutus is the apprehension
of a world of suffering figures, of great philosophic
verse: of the shepherd Michael, of the afflicted
Margaret, of certain poems of Rossetti and Patmore
and others.

The other entrance is, in one word, Donne; in
two words, the Metaphysicals. In them the specula-
tive intellect is made one with poetry. Donne spoke
of the lady whose body thought; but his own mind
felt. His own intellectual emotion discovered her
corporeal intelligence. Keats enters directly on
greatness; Donne and Marvell find it by a longer
road, passing over the mountains of the mind. But
they do find it. At their beginning lie such lyrics as

'Go and catch a falling star'—single and delightful things. These simplicities are often daintily or fantastically attired, so that they go in a kind of solemn state; a curious capacity for this was in Lamb, in those curious poems *A Farewell to Tobacco* and *On an Infant dying as soon as born.* They proceed to real exploration; they are more difficult than the simple lyrists but, being more subtle, they are more exact. Marvell's *To his Coy Mistress* is not only more strange than Waller's *Go, lovely Rose*; it is also a much finer and truer imagination. It contains all the beauty as well as all the peril of delay, and the fatal ironic and threatening meiosis of

> The grave's a fine and private place,
> But none, I think, do there embrace

might terrify his mistress to a surrender which Waller could only implore.

The anonymous author of

> When Molly smiles beneath her cow
> I feel my heart I can't tell how

gave us a just sense of an 'unknown mode of being'. But

> My love is of a birth as rare
>   As 'tis for object strange and high;
> It was begotten by Despair
>   Upon Impossibility—

that is that unknown made known, the architecture of young romantic love, the hiding-place of its power, recognized in a flash and with the glory of poetry. Once at least Marvell went even farther and touched greatness, in the death of the King—

> But bowed his comely head
> Down, as upon a bed.

Donne, who was a greater poet, did it more completely. Where Tennyson wrote one line 'In the spring a young man's fancy lightly turns to thoughts of love' Donne analysed and discovered that strange fact in *Love's Growth* ('I scarce believe to be so pure'). If his poetry does not contain it invites subversion—'Batter my heart, three-personed God'; its terror seems sometimes to be caused by the absence of an overthrow which it at once fears and desires. But also, at the other end of its path, it found greatness: the proof is in

> Wilt thou forgive that sin where I begun
> Which was my sin though it were done before;

right on to the utter peace of

> When thou hast done that Thou has done;
> I ask no more.

The Metaphysicals are sometimes spoken of as if they were a rare, almost an esoteric, school of poetry. But in effect they are natural to our genius, and many an English poet is related to them. To begin with a flea and end with God is almost the habit of English verse; though both the flea and God are sometimes—as in Shakespeare—given different names. Certainly that great group closed in high philosophic poetry.

The power which poetry now has is a power to search out such things, and to search them out in us. It has power to search, but, having done this, it has power on us to cause what it does to be 'felt in the blood and felt along the heart'. Actually, of course, this way of putting it is untrue, for its power of searching and of communicating is one; it is poetry. But poetry is now beginning to exist precisely in 'the hiding-places of man's power'; we find them in the poetry, and as the poetry fills us, we find them in ourselves. We understand our own architecture; the sense of our capacity for a unity of experience is aroused, and there exists what Arnold remotely called 'a criticism of life'—a knowledge, a judgement of life 'with glory'.

But there is another possibility, another task for poetry to undertake—the discovery of subversion. 'The wondrous architecture' is studied; but if that architecture was itself overthrown? It is in such an overthrow that there exists chiefly 'a conflict of sensations without name'; this human experience must also be the subject of poetry, this also must be recognized 'in flashes and with glory not its own'. The study of lesser poetry has done, perhaps, exactly what Wordsworth said the reading of faery-tales and romances had done for him; when from the depths of our nature the dead thing is dragged up, with

> ghastly face, a spectre shape
> Of terror,

it is still possible to know it in poetry. Poetry at least must know it composedly, harmoniously, and it does so, not in any way by lessening the terror, but by exploring it to its utmost, by noting detail and using detail. Troilus and Othello, Lear and Satan, Wordsworth himself in the village church, are not in the least vague figures. If the intense genius of the poets had not endured to know the extremest contradiction of that rent and outraged nature which is their subject we should have had—not Satan but a larger Comus, not Othello but a dimmer Brutus. To discover it Milton raised his blank verse to a new power; Shakespeare used a new power in a new style. The thing inseparate exists. Around that discovery the unchanging greatness of Wordsworth moves in a flowing circle of noble verse, tender, courageous, profound, ever aware of catastrophe and solitude and of possibilities within them, but never—more than that once—quite fathoming them by its poetry alone. Even so, his poetry gives us something which, had he been greater, we should not have had—the sense of that vision, the steady sweep of verse which looks at the depths and is not alarmed. It turns from them nobly; it follows, like the speech of the Leech-Gatherer, 'in solemn order, With something of a lofty utterance drest'. Milton's poetry is far more the knowledge of the thing. Wordsworth, as it were, took Milton for his subject. To say that Milton took Shakespeare as his would be too brave a generalization. But his poetry does at least discover the self-consciousness of the mind in which the conflict of sensations rages; that conflict which Shakespeare's poetry purely and absolutely discovered. Milton accepted—what Shakespeare in *Troilus* and *Measure for Measure* refused—the artistic method of confronting moral values in almost equally great impersonations. If Shakespeare utters moral judgements they are to be deduced; they are not verbally explicit. But Milton's are, and they are a part of his greatness. What other English imagination could have discovered both the intense distress of Adam at the prospect of being parted from Eve (ix, 886–999)—

'to lose thee were to lose myself'—and what follows?
Adam takes the fruit in an agony of love and despair;
it is more than the world, it is heaven, well lost for
love. And then, unlike our weak romantic applause,
Milton's imagination by its sheer strength, having
perfectly understood so much devotion, denounces
it—

> such compliance *bad*
> Such recompense best merits.

It would be inhuman, if it were not Milton. But
Milton is never inhuman.

The mystery of reconciliation which this divided
poetry found for itself at the end of *Samson* is the close
of Milton's knowledge of mankind: he never discovered simplicity. How Shakespeare went beyond
him has already been suggested. In that same passage
on the crossing of the Alps Wordsworth says that the
soul (and I think that throughout the *Prelude* when
Wordsworth says 'the soul' the lines are usually
applicable to poetry), that

> the soul
> Seeks for no trophies, struggles for no spoils
> That may attest her prowesss, blest in thoughts
> That are their own perfection and reward,
> Strong in herself and in beatitude
> That hides her.

The closing of Shakespeare's genius is our great
example of this. After *Hamlet* it had absented itself
from felicity, and in the plays that concluded his
working life it is something other than felicity which
seems to return. Felicity for the characters, perhaps,
but for us Wordsworth's word is preferable—beatitude; they are the beatitude of poetry. Shakespeare

CONCLUSION   211

himself may or may not have been happy. But there
is about those last plays something which is at a
little distance from us; they are difficult fully to
apprehend, being clear as crystal. Leontes is so
simply (not merely) jealous; Imogen is so simply
brave and beautiful; Miranda is so simply loving;
Autolycus is so simply a rascal; even Paulina is
simply 'a good woman': the country is so much the
country, the court so much the court, the magical
island of Prospero so greatly enchanted: Caliban is
so perfectly sub-human and Ariel so nearly non-
human. There are no more unknown modes of being;
all things are subject to poetic power. The thought is
so impersonated that there is no division between
image and vital soul. It is at ease in Zion. But it is in
Zion that it is at ease, and perhaps that Zion is as far
beyond our normal instructed poetic intelligence as
Milton is beyond the young poetic delight that feeds
on Macaulay or Scott. No other of our poets has so
wholly attained to such a final simplicity; and this,
among so much else, is his greatness—that in him the
poetic genius perfectly, or at least to the greatest
perfection that we can imagine, fulfilled itself. Other
poets had purposed it—'the two great ends of
liberty and power'; 'and justify the ways of God to
men'. Other poets had praised the greatness of
poetry—indirectly or directly.

Thou wast not born for death, immortal bird!

I am the eye with which the universe
Beholds itself and knows itself divine.

But perhaps there is no lovelier vision in which, at
a distance, the lesser poetry beholds the greater than

Arnold's, when after Empedocles had flung himself into the crater of Etna the voice of the young Greek singer is heard floating up the mountain, in a prophecy of poetry upon its way to its Olympian conclusion.

Through the black, rushing smoke-bursts,
Thick breaks the red flame;
All Etna heaves fiercely
Her forest-cloth'd frame.

Not here, O Apollo!
Are haunts meet for thee.
But, where Helicon breaks down
In cliff to the sea,

Where the moon-silver'd inlets
Send far their light voice
Up the still vale of Thisbe,
O speed, and rejoice!

On the sward at the cliff-top
Lie strewn the white flocks;
On the cliff-side the pigeons
Roost deep in the rocks.

In the moonlight the shepherds,
Soft lull'd by the rills,
Lie wrapt in their blankets,
Asleep on the hills.

—What forms are these coming
So white through the gloom?
What garments out-glistening
The gold-flower'd broom?

What sweet-breathing presence
Out-perfumes the thyme?
What voices enrapture
The night's balmy prime?—

'Tis Apollo comes leading
His choir, the Nine.
—The leader is fairest,
But all are divine.

They are lost in the hollows!
They stream up again!
What seeks on this mountain
The glorified train?—

They bathe on this mountain,
In the spring by their road;
Then on to Olympus,
Their endless abode!

—Whose praise do they mention?
Of what is it told?—
What will be for ever;
What was from of old.

First hymn they the Father
Of all things; and then
The rest of immortals,
The action of men.

The day in his hotness,
The strife with the palm;
The night in her silence,
The stars in their calm.

APPENDIX

CHRONOLOGICAL LIST OF SHAKESPEARE'S PLAYS

1590–1
2 Henry VI
3 Henry VI

1591–2
1 Henry VI

1592–3
Richard III
Comedy of Errors

1593–4
Titus Andronicus
Taming of the Shrew

1594–5
Two Gentlemen of Verona
Love's Labour's Lost
Romeo and Juliet

1595–6
Richard II
Midsummer-Night's Dream

1596–7
King John
Merchant of Venice

1597–8
1 Henry IV
2 Henry IV

1598–9
Much Ado About Nothing
Henry V

1599–1600
Julius Caesar
As You Like It
Twelfth Night

1600–1
Hamlet
Merry Wives of Windsor

1601–2
Troilus and Cressida

1602–3
All's Well That Ends Well

1603–4
—

1604–5
Measure for Measure
Othello

1605–6
King Lear
Macbeth

1606–7
Antony and Cleopatra

1607–8
Coriolanus
Timon of Athens

1608–9
Pericles

1609–10
Cymbeline

1610–11
Winter's Tale

1611–12
Tempest

1612–13
Henry VIII
Two Noble Kinsmen